TWAYNE'S WORLD AUTHORS SERIES
A Survey of the World's Literature

CANADA

Canadian Fiction

TWAS 630

CANADIAN FICTION

By JOSEPH and JOHANNA JONES

University of Texas, Austin

TWAYNE PUBLISHERS
A DIVISION OF G.K. HALL & CO., BOSTON

Library of Congress Cataloging in Publication Data

Jones, Joseph Jay, 1908–
Canadian Fiction

(Twayne's world authors series ; TWAS 630 : Canada)
Bibliography: p. 152–73
Includes Index.
1. Canadian Fiction—History and criticism.
I. Jones, Johanna, joint author. II. Title.
PR9192.2.J6 813'.009'971 80-29092
ISBN 0-8057-6473-9

Contents

About the Authors

Joseph and Johanna Jones, both native Nebraskans, arrived in Austin, Texas, in 1935. Dr. Jones at that time joined the English staff at the University of Texas where he is now Professor Emeritus. Mrs. Jones was a student at the University and later taught in the Austin schools in addition to writing book reviews. In 1953 a Fulbright assignment took the family, now five, to New Zealand. Subsequently they went to South Africa (1960–61) and Hong Kong (1965–66) where Professor Jones lectured.

Professor Jones has contributed to various journals and edited *American Literary Manuscripts* (1960), *Image of Australia* (1962), and *WLWE Newsletter* (1962–70), together with upwards of fifty volumes for Twayne's World Authors Series, concerning authors from Australia, Canada, Africa, New Zealand, and the West Indies. His books include *The Cradle of Erewhon: Samuel Butler in New Zealand* (1959), *Terranglia: the Case for English as World-Literature* (1965), a small volume of poems entitled *Handful of Hong Kong* (1966), several other similar volumes of "seventeener" (free-style haiku) poems of various dates, and *Radical Cousins: Nineteenth Century American & Australian Writers* (1976).

The Joneses have worked together in various library collections in England, Australia, and elsewhere for some fifteen years or more on what they choose to call "World English." This volume on Canadian fiction and two companion volumes on Australian and New Zealand fiction, in press, are among the fruits of this collaboration. The Joneses continue to enjoy travelling, especially by ship, and hope to make several more voyages on whatever type of seagoing craft remains available.

Preface

A recent (1967) anthology of Canadian poetry bears this interesting title: *The Poetry of the Canadian People: Two Hundred Years of Hard Work*. If the reader should think that the volume in hand on the fiction of the Canadian people might be subtitled, in compensation, "two hundred years of fun and games," let him be warned by this statement from Margaret Atwood's *Survival* (1972):

> ...Canadian gloom is more unrelieved than most and the death and failure toll out of proportion. Given a choice of the negative or positive aspects of any symbol—sea as life-giving Mother, sea as what your ship goes down in; tree as symbol of growth, tree as what falls on your head—Canadians show a marked preference for the negative.

Canadian fiction is not quite all unrelieved gloom, however, as the work of Stephen Leacock serves immediately to convince us. It is in fact an interesting mixture of all sorts of moods, motifs, and styles. After two hundred years of growth and change, the future of Canadian fiction appears to be fairly well assured.

Our purpose in providing this introductory volume is to reveal to the reader a dimension of literature in English with which, more than likely, he is not yet very familiar. To the austere shade of Matthew Arnold, who once asked contemptuously, "Are we to have a primer of Canadian literature, too, and a primer of Australian?" we are obliged to reply, "Yes, Mr. Arnold, these do seem necessary at least until there is more culture and less anarchy relating to the study of English on the global basis than has so far been achieved." For guidance and assistance we are grateful to have been able to rely on the work of Canadian critics and scholars, especially those whose books and articles have appeared in refreshing abundance during the past ten to fifteen years. Aware that a historical survey of some length and depth would enhance the approach to fiction, but confined by limitations of space, we have tried to let the fiction itself furnish as much of the Canadian background as we could contrive, assisted by a preliminary chronology. Canadian authors, of late, have been much interviewed or invited to contribute special comment on their work; references to the published results of such interesting encounters appear after the names of some thirty different writers of fiction listed in the bibliography, along with other selected criticism.

Since this book is part of an extensive series whose ultimate aim is to examine the whole corpus of world literature, some awareness of relationships to other writing in English should naturally be expected. For Canadian writers, these relationships are felt most strongly (though not in the same ways) in the vast literatures of the British Isles and the United States. The best Canadian criticism today is aware of not only these international analogues and parallels, but of others in the Commonwealth—Australia and New Zealand, for example, and the West Indies. Some of all this, at least, we have tried here and there to suggest.

Efforts to see interrelations between contemporary writers as well as to look at the literary-historical sequence are commencing to appear. A notable example is Warren Tallman's "Wolf in the Snow," in *Canadian Literature* (Summer 1960), which takes five novels—Sinclair Ross's *As For Me and My House*, W. O. Mitchell's *Who Has Seen the Wind*, Hugh MacLennan's *Each Man's Son*, Ernest Buckler's *The Mountain and the Valley*, and Mordecai Richler's *The Apprenticeship of Duddy Kravitz*—as "worth close consideration by those who take the visions of fiction as a decisive mode of relatedness to the actual house in which we live."

If as Margaret Laurence—and other Canadian writers—believe "the change [since 1960] in the whole cultural situation in Canada has been enormous," there is every good reason for emphasizing recent fiction. To what degree is it an outgrowth of earlier tendencies, and to what degree something altogether new? About this, there is bound to be much room for disagreement; but we think it is reasonable to concede that present-day Canadian fiction has achieved distinction largely on the basis of previous efforts, many of them (though certainly not all) of less distinction, and that the whole process needs to be examined.

We are grateful to the staffs of several libraries in which the work for this volume has been done, especially those of the University of Texas at Austin, the University of London, and other London collections at Canada House, the Commonwealth Institute, and the Royal Commonwealth Society. Special thanks are owing, as well, to Vivienne Dickson and John Sherrill for help in preparing the manuscript for publication.

JOSEPH AND JOHANNA JONES

Austin, Texas

Chronology

This chronology includes only landmark dates in Canadian political and social history, together with approximately seventy titles of novels or books of stories and some important scholarly works and periodicals. It is intended to indicate, for the most part, the first appearances of authors whose works represent shifts in literary direction or are otherwise historically significant; thus it is not, in any sense, a listing of all the "most important" works of Canadian fiction. For more detailed information on authors and titles, the reader should consult the appended bibliography.

?	Undated early visits by Norsemen and possibly other Europeans
1497	John Cabot's discovery of Newfoundland (not claimed for Britain until 1583)
1598–1600	Richard Hakluyt's *Principal Navigations* which contains accounts of voyages to Canada
1610	Hudson's explorations (Hudson and James Bays)
1632	*The Jesuit Relations* (records of missions in Great Lakes area)
1670	Hudson's Bay Company chartered
1713	Treaty of Utrecht, by which France yields Hudson Bay, Newfoundland, and Acadia to Britain
1749	Halifax founded (first printing press 1751, establishment of *Halifax Gazette* 1752)
1755–1763	British-French hostilities including expulsion of Acadians, Seven Years' War, Treaty of Paris giving Britain control of most formerly French territories in North America
1769	Frances Brooke's *The History of Emily Montague;* "first" Canadian novel
1774	Quebec Act
1776	Declaration of Independence and beginning of American Revolution

1783   End of American Revolution, emigration of United Empire Loyalists

1791   Constitutional Act, separating Upper Canada (later Ontario) from Lower Canada (later Quebec)

1812–   British war with United States
1814

1821   Thomas McCulloch's *Letters of Mephibosheth Stepsure* (in *Acadian Recorder*, 1821–23)

1823   *The Canadian Magazine* established in Montreal (published one year only)

1824   Julia Beckwith's *St. Ursula's Convent*

1827   Joseph Howe becomes proprietor of the *Nova Scotian*

1830   John Galt's *Lawrie Todd*

1832   John Richardson's *Wacousta*

1836   Catherine Parr Traill's *The Backwoods of Canada*; Thomas Chandler Haliburton's *The Clockmaker* (first series)

1837   Rebellions in both Upper and Lower Canada, followed by Durham Report 1839 and union of the Canadas 1841

1838   *The Literary Garland* established (published until 1851)

1846   Britain abandons claims to Oregon

1852   Susanna Moodie's *Roughing It in the Bush*; *Canadian Journal* established (published until 1878)

1856   R. M. Ballantyne's *The Young Fur Traders*

1865   Charles Heavysege's *The Advocate*

1866   Fenian Raids across Canadian border (by Irish from U. S.)

1867   British North America Act, creating Dominion of Canada with Sir John MacDonald first Prime Minister; U. S. Alaska purchase

1869–   First Riel (Red River) Rebellion
1871

1871   Alexander Begg's *Dot-it-Down*

1877   William Kirby's *The Golden Dog*

1882   Royal Society of Canada founded

1885   Second Riel Rebellion (Riel hanged)

1886   Canadian Pacific Railway completed

1888   James DeMille's *A Strange Manuscript Found in a Copper Cylinder*

1892   Gilbert Parker's *Pierre and His People*

1893   *Queen's Quarterly* established

1894   Marshall Saunders's *Beautiful Joe*
1895   E.W. Thomson's *Old Man Savarin*
1896   Charles G. D. Roberts's *Earth's Enigmas;* Duncan Campbell Scott's *In The Village of Viger*
1897   Klondike Gold Rush
1898   Ralph Connor's *Black Rock;* Ernest Thompson Seton's *Wild Animals I Have Known*
1904   Sara Jeannette Duncan's *The Imperialist*
1908   Nellie L. McClung's *Sowing Seeds in Danny;* L. M. Montgomery's *Anne of Green Gables*
1910   Stephen Leacock's *Literary Lapses*
1912   Sinking of *Titanic*
1914–   World War I
1918
1915   Arthur J. Stringer's *The Prairie Wife*
1920   *Canadian Forum* established
1921   *Dalhousie Review* established; Canadian Authors Association formed
1922   F. P. Grove's *Over Prairie Trails*
1923   Laura Salverson's *The Viking Heart*
1925   Martha Ostenso's *Wild Geese*
1926   Robert Stead's *Grain*
1927   Mazo de la Roche's *Jalna*
1928   Morley Callaghan's *Strange Fugitive;* Raymond Knister's edition of *Canadian Short Stories*
1929   Raymond Knister's *White Narcissus*
1931   *University of Toronto Quarterly* established
1936   Phillip Child's *God's Sparrows*
1937   Governor General's Literary Awards established
1939   Irene Baird's *Waste Heritage*
1939–   World War II
1945
1941   Hugh MacLennan's *Barometer Rising;* Sinclair Ross's *As for Me and My House*
1942   Thomas Raddall's *His Majesty's Yankees*
1944   Gwethalyn Graham's *Earth and High Heaven*
1946   Ralph Allen's *Home Made Banners;* Selwyn Dewdny's *Wind Without Rain*
1947   Paul Hiebert's *Sarah Binks;* Malcolm Lowry's *Under the Volcano;* E. M. McCourt's *Music at the Close;* W. O.

Mitchell's *Who Has Seen the Wind;* Ethel Wilson's *Hetty Dorval*

1948 Henry Kreisel's *The Rich Man*

1949 Earle Birney's *Turvey;* Hugh Garner's *Storm Below*

1951 Ernest Buckler's *The Mountain and the Valley;* Robertson Davies's *Tempest-Tost;* A. M. Klein's *The Second Scroll*

1952 Norman Levine's *The Angled Road*

1953 First year of the Stratford (Ont.) Festival

1954 Mordecai Richler's *The Acrobats*

1956 Fred Bodsworth's *The Last of the Curlews;* Mavis Gallant's *The Other Paris;* Adele Wiseman's *The Sacrifice*

1957 Canada Council established

1959 Sheila Watson's *The Double Hook; Canadian Literature* established

1960 Margaret Laurence's *This Side Jordan;* Brian Moore's *The Luck of Ginger Coffey*

1962 Hugh Hood's *Flying A Red Kite and Other Stories*

1963 Leonard Cohen's *The Favourite Game*

1964 Douglas LePan's *The Deserter*

1965 *Literary History of Canada,* ed. C. F. Klinck

1966 Robert Kroetsch's *The Words of My Roaring*

1967 Expo 67: centenary of Confederation

1968 Jack Ludwig's *Above Ground*

1969 Margaret Atwood's *The Edible Woman;* Gwendolyn McEwen's *The Shadow Maker*

1970 Marian Engel's *The Honeyman Festival;* Rudy Wiebe's *The Blue Mountains of China*

1971 Ronald Lee's *Goddam Gypsy*

1972 David Godfrey's *The New Ancestors;* John Metcalf's *Going Down Slow*

CHAPTER 1

Brooke to Richardson

Self-appraisal now begins to reveal, among other things, that the Canadian writers of the past must have been much more perceptive, more prophetic and disenchanted, than their readers have guessed. In the land which pretends to have no ghosts, they have seen ghosts; in the country without a mythology, they have heard the ground bass of myth; in a country born not of love and struggle but of politics, they have fought battles; and, with reserve and irony, they have offered their country love.

—Robertson Davies

ANYONE fortunate enough to have visited Montreal's "Expo 67" during Canada's centennial year—the anniversary of Dominion status within what, as of 1867, was the British Empire and is now the Commonwealth—came away with a feeling of having realized for perhaps the first time the magnitude and great beauty of physical Canada as well as the diversity and—upon occasion—the intensity of her people. One can say "intensity" advisedly, for whatever her reputation may be for conservative, comparatively low-key views and behavior, it is a fact that Canada has seen more uprisings against British rule, more declared and undeclared civil wars, than has her neighbor to the south—not on the same scale, to be sure, but nonetheless bona fide gestures of protest. After World War II, the historical divisions between French– and English–speaking Canadians again became acute, remaining turbulently unsettled into the 1970s.

Since conditions of this sort are proverbially interesting to writers, we can expect to encounter in Canadian fiction all sorts of rivalries and conflicts. These are both collective and personal, ranging from small-town squabbles to involvements on the international scale. As critics sometimes see it, such rivalries and conflicts involve the "search for Canadian identity" and other deep-seated psychological urges.

Parts of "Man and His World" exhibit could still be viewed in Montreal a decade after 1967, though of course not in the whole original format: a tribute to the quality of the original perform- ance which set new goals for succeeding expositions and intro- duced a whole new tone into the enterprise of staging them, much the same way as Prince Albert's "Great Exhibition" of 1851 gave rise to a series of emulators. It was made clear in Montreal and in satellite celebrations that Canadian authors did have a country well worth writing about; and since then both the quantity and quality of Canadian literature have continued to rise, in French and English alike. There has been, moreover, a lively critical response to such quickening. In the chapters to follow we shall be looking at the course of English Canadian fiction from its begin- nings in the mid-eighteenth century onward through 1975, re- membering that French Canada has its own story to tell.

Early Canadian writing resembles early American, in the topics it treats as well as in its level of literary quality. Neither, in fact, has a very strong claim to be called literature in the strict sense, for North America—the gradually deepening eastern rind of it throughout the seventeenth and early eighteenth centuries—was all colonial territory, although not until the 1760s did it belong to a single colonial power. And like colonists in other parts of the world, British or otherwise, the people who lived there were for the most part too busy making history to think of recording more than a few notes in their diaries or of writing elaborate letters home to Europe. Nor was it expected that they would: only a limited number could write or read, and those who could were too much occupied, along with their fellows, to form even the beginnings of a literary class. Exceptions to this general rule were the clergymen, charged with reading and writing for the proper care of their congregations, and the magistrates, makers and interpreters of laws, such as were needed or could be framed apart from directives from the home country. Consequently, most early writing, sacred and secular alike, was utilitarian.

European political events, as well as the general state of European culture, had a heavy bearing upon what was done in the colonies and who was sent to do it. The 1640s and 50s saw England convulsed in civil war, the earlier part of the century having led up to it and the remainder devoted to attempts at reconstruction which had varying success. It was not a time for systematic, peaceful penetration into the New World; and even before, the wise and compassionate Frenchman Montaigne had found occasion to lament the brutality and stupidity with which Europe had commenced its despoliation of a natural paradise inhabited by a brave and generous people, as he viewed events. But that did not deter the conquerors, possessors, and publicists from representing conditions of settlement as dependent upon subduing the natives by means ranging from introducing them into communal Christianity to policies not far from Kurtzian "Exterminate all the brutes!" Convert or exterminate, as you please, and then it will be yours to inherit and enjoy an earthly paradise: such was the dream.

The documents reflecting all stages between these two extremes are the stuff of history and of historical fiction at the same time: voyagers' accounts expanded from ships' logs, by or about trips to Newfoundland or elsewhere, made by the Cabots, Frobisher, Wyet, Leigh, and Gilbert. These, and the ballads which sometimes chronicled less precisely the same exploits, were chiefly narrative: proto-fiction, then, was first upon the scene, as we would expect it to be. Once settlement was attempted and enjoyed any lasting success, narratives of pioneering began to appear, filled with snowflakes in the winter, mosquitoes in the summer, and promotional optimism at all seasons. Frenchmen in New France, by contrast, were producing such monuments as the *Jesuit Relations* and other manifestations of Catholic culture which was resolved to stay put, as the beginnings of theater may suggest.

Special circumstances, set in motion almost immediately following the transfer of power from France to Britain in the 1760s, produced a movement out of the northernmost of the original thirteen colonies into Nova Scotia, New Brunswick, and the Niagara region when thousands of Loyalists were forced to migrate at the end of the American Revolution. Many of these people, though by no means all, were literate and more than ready to express themselves on the subject of their hardships. Prose narratives and collections of letters were published from the early 1780s to as late as 1901, the most substantial being those of James Moody, Edward Winslow, and Jacob Bailey. Much the same story of Loyalist difficulties was revealed in the poetry of Joseph Stansbury and Jonathan Odell.

Jacob Bailey's narrative, *The Frontier Missionary* (1853), is in the line of religious histories and personal reminiscences that form a Protestant counterpart to the earlier *Jesuit Relations*. The most outstanding of these is *The Life and Journal of the Rev. Mr. Henry Alline* (1806), which for its Calvinistic piety has been compared with Jonathan Edwards's *Personal Narrative* in the preceding century, just as it might be with Edward Eggleston's circuit-riding novels in the next, for its graphic descriptions of frontier religion. The Reverend Joshua Marsden, an English parson who spent the years 1799–1807 as a missionary in the Maritime Provinces, wrote both prose and verse accounts of his experiences; his verse, says the poet-critic Fred Cogswell, "is superior to his prose and shows considerable talent; it fails to achieve its potential excellence mainly because Marsden kept it ever subordinate to his primary calling as a publicist for the Methodist church."[1] Nor did Canada lack an early religious parallel to Anne Bradstreet of Massachusetts; *A Narrative of the Life and Christian Experience of Mrs. Mary Bradley* (1849) relates to a period in Mrs. Bradley's life (she was born in 1771) "on a frontier where the chief source of interest, apart from daily routine, was the sermons preached by such men as Henry Alline, James MacGregor, and Joshua Marsden."[2]

Travel literature, a growing source of interest to Europeans and at times a source of profit to the writer, shows several dimensions within the half century between the Treaty of Paris (1763) and the War of 1812. There are, for instance, an Indian-captivity narrative by Thomas Ridout (written in the 1780s but not published until 1890), and other local history by Ridout and his two sons, along with business journeys of fur traders and other merchants (the most notable of these accounts is by Alexander Henry of Montreal, *Travels and Adventures in Canada and the Indian Territories between the Years 1760 and 1776*, published 1809). Other more or less professional travellers' works, by visitors or temporary residents, include: George Heriot's *Travels Through the Canadas* (1807), Isaac Weld, Jr.'s *Travels* through both the new United States and Canada in the later 1790s, and John Lambert's *Travels* of ten years later. Lambert was at least aware that the arts already existed in Canada albeit in a rudimentary form, as shown by a contemptuous account of theatricals in Quebec and the general observation that "The state of literature and the arts did not improve very rapidly after the conquest of the country by the English."[3] Such books as these are useful source-works for historians, but quite apart from that function they also serve the historical novelist, dramatist, and poet (for example, E.J. Pratt or Margaret Atwood).

I *Frances Brooke*

When *The History of Emily Montague* appeared in England in 1769, its author, Frances Brooke, was a young matron aged thirty-five, wife of an army chaplain stationed at Quebec. She had already begun a literary career at home, editing a periodical, writing a play, and publishing her first novel, *The History of Julia Mandeville*, in 1763, the year she joined her husband in Canada. Despite Lambert's deprecating remarks about the slowness of artistic development, fiction of Canadian origin—by virtue of Mrs. Brooke's presence for five years in the 1760s—appeared a full generation before the American novel came upon the scene: in the early dawn of English fiction itself, contemporaneous with Richardson, Fielding, Smollett, and Sterne.

Emily Montague, which is written in the form of letters, resembles Samuel Richardson's novels more closely than those of any of the others in the quartet just named. There is ample warrant for the method in the fact that three pairs of lovers (the principals are Emily Montague and Colonel Rivers) and some nonromantic characters are separated by the Atlantic Ocean and St. Lawrence River, a circumstance that motivates also a good bit of the description and social commentary mortised into the plot. These samples from the love-epistles (there are many interminable ones, very much the same) will afford a brief glimpse at the style; the first is by Emily, writing about Colonel Rivers, and the second is by Rivers, writing about Emily.

He is formed to charm the soul of woman; his delicacy, his sensibility, the mind that speaks through those eloquent eyes; the thousand graces of his air, the sound of his voice—my dear, I never heard him speak without feeling a softness of which it is impossible to convey an idea.

She is an angel, my dear Lucy [the writer's sister], and no words can do her justice: I am the happiest of mankind; . . . . her looks, her air, her tone of voice, her blushes, her very silence—how could I ever doubt her tenderness? have not those lovely eyes a thousand times betrayed the dear secret of her heart?[4]

Fortunately, for most readers, such epistles are interspersed with others from Emily's coquettish friend Arabella Fermor (the name from Pope's "Rape of the Lock" set, perhaps?) and from her father, Captain William Fermor, whose reports develop the social and political background. Writing to an unnamed English earl, Captain Fermor delivers himself, more than once, of such unflattering opinions as these:

> Nothing can be more true, my Lord, than that poverty is ever the inseparable companion of indolence.
> I see proofs of it every moment before me; with a soil fruitful beyond all belief, the Canadians are poor on lands which are their own property. . . .
> This indolence appears in every thing. . . .[5]

The same note is to be heard in later generations, well past the turn of the nineteenth century, from such moralists as Thomas McCulloch and Thomas Chandler Haliburton.

II   Thomas McCulloch

Scottish names are prevalent in Canadian literature and politics alike. While there was never quite a Burns or a Scott in early poetry and fiction, one Scots Presbyterian minister, Thomas McCulloch, possessed enough of a literary urge to write sketches challenging the interpretations of Presbyterianism in Scott's *Old Mortality* but was unable to find a publisher for them. He did publish, at Edinburgh in 1826, a brace of stories under the title *William and Melville*, largely given over to showing the evils of drink in early Halifax. (Thomas McCulloch's congregation was at Pictou, N.S.) Thus failing, for the most part, to win an audience in his native Scotland, McCulloch turned to a local paper, the *Acadian Recorder*, where *The Letters of Mephibosheth Stepsure* appeared in the early 1820s but were not seen in book form until 1860, years after the death of the author.

Fred Cogswell, who lives in the region and writes about it in our day, observes that there is "much to repel" a twentieth-century reader in the character that McCulloch created: Stepsure, true to his name, achieves a "plodding rise to respectability and affluence [starting from a crippled orphanhood] in the community of Pictou by a combination of hard work, abstinence, religiosity, and cunning," in contrast to many of his fellow citizens who go the way of drink and depravity.

Christian ethics, one feels, ought to be an end in themselves and not a means of making money, and to a healthy nature cold-blooded gloating over the misfortunes and failures of others is never pleasant. The book also has technical flaws. The characters—Trot, Whinge, Sham, Clippet—are, as their names suggest, caricatures; the episodes are often farce; and the use again and again of the same plot situations is monotonous. To compensate for these defects [the series of sixteen letters *in toto*] possess a marvellously unified tone and sensibility, a robust realism, a lack of prudishness, and a sustained, almost Swiftian, irony.[6]

Stepsure's story of Ehud Slush, farmer turned fox trapper, illustrates the author's sarcastic disapproval of all who think there is an easy road to success:

About twelve years ago, Slush was a good-natured young fellow. In due time, according to the practice of our town, he married and settled upon a lot of good land, and really had the prospect of being very comfortable. He had never, indeed, been guilty of hard work; but, now, he had got a wife in addition to his mare; and working or starving were his only alternatives. Ehud boldly chose the first, sharpened his axe, and determined that no son of the forest should resist its strokes.[7]

Slush soon forgets his resolves and imagines he can do better by trapping. Predictably, he fails to stay solvent and is soon barely one jump—if always that—ahead of the sheriff, Mr. Catchem. In a tongue-in-cheek conclusion, Stepsure points out:

The country needs labor, and catching foxes is a laborious trade. . . . For my own part, I wish the trade encouraged; and, therefore, give notice to all fox catchers, that by and by, when they want potatoes, or begin to wonder about the scarcity of cash, my cousin Harrow has the first for sale; and Mr. Catchem will tell them about the last.[8]

Northrop Frye sees McCulloch as "the founder of genuine Canadian humour," by which is meant humor "which is based on a vision of society and is not merely a series of wisecracks on a single theme."

McCulloch makes it clear that by simple living he does not mean poverty,

still less a mode of life that excludes cultivating the mind. Like the man in
Robert Frost, Stepsure believes that good fences make good neighbors,
although there are references to his willingness to help such neighbors as
are not mere spongers.[9]

The same critic, in a different connection, makes some remarks on
religion as a force in Canadian literature which might well be
applied to McCulloch and the generation succeeding him:

Leacock has a story which I often turn to because the particular aspect of
Canadian culture it reflects has never been more accurately caught. He
tells of the rivalry in an Ontario town between two preachers, one
Anglican and the other Presbyterian. The latter taught ethics in the local
college on weekdays—without salary—and preached on Sundays. He
gave his students, says Leacock, three parts Hegel and two parts St. Paul,
and on Sunday he reversed the dose and gave his parishioners three parts
St. Paul and two parts Hegel. Religion has been a major—perhaps the
major—cultural force in Canada, at least down to the last generation or
two. The churches not only influenced the cultural climate but took an
active part in the production of poetry and fiction, as the popularity of
Ralph Connor reminds us. But the effective religious factors in Canada
were doctrinal and evangelical, those that stressed the arguments of
religion at the expense of its imagery.[10]

Stepsure is the sort of literary personality to be kept in mind, as
we shall discover in our journey among Canadian fictional
characters well down into our century. Very frequently indeed
these are concerned about their neighbors' business, sometimes
self-righteously, other times sarcastically or (less often) sympathetically. The plains of Manitoba and Alberta will produce them as
abundantly as the backwoods of Ontario or the longer-settled
Maritimes. Turning the other way, we hear in such didactic prose
as *The Stepsure Letters* distinct echoes of the Addisonian eighteenth century, perhaps even the colonial part of it as in Benjamin
Franklin's *Dogood Papers* or *Poor Richard's Almanac.* At the same
time it points forward to Thomas Chandler Haliburton, who in
the next decade was to take over much the same tradition and give
it new strength.

III   *Julia Catherine Hart*

With a temporary resident like Frances Brooke having given so
animated a view of early Canada, one might expect that a native-

born writer could at least approach the same standard, but such was not the case: of Julia Catherine Hart's *St. Ursula's Convent; or, the Nun of Canada* (1824) the most that literary historians have to say is that its "sole claim to attention is that it was the first work of fiction to be written by a native-born English-speaking Canadian and the first to be published in what is now Canada."[11] The following year, Mrs. Hart's *Tonnewonte; or, the Adopted Son of America* was published at Watertown, New York. This novel, still dealing with fashionable society, takes up a theme that had been common in British literature throughout the eighteenth century and indeed before that—the corrupting influence of Continental manners, especially French and (earlier) Italian. Following the American Revolution, political reasons (at least in part) had prompted Royall Tyler's comedy *The Contrast* (1787) which contrasted effete English (really general European) society with the new and preferable democratic American simplicity. Even so, Mrs. Hart, as Norah Story says, "took a big step for a writer of romance in her day by looking beyond her immediate environment and by constructing a plot designed to show that life in North America with its simplicity was superior to that of the wealthy European circles."[12]

IV   *John Richardson*

Shortly after Mrs. Hart's *Tonnewonte* Major John Richardson, publishing in London, attempted unsuccessfully a similar critique of European profligacy in *Écarté; or the Salons of Paris* (1829). Richardson, Whose literary career like his personal appearance and the tone of his writings bears more than casual resemblance to Edgar Allan Poe, was the earliest English Canadian man of letters, having written poetry, drama, fiction, history, and autobiography before his death in obscurity in New York City (1852). Like Poe, he was stormy in his personal relationships, unsettled in residence, and much addicted to gothicism. *Wacousta* (1832), the one work he is best remembered for, until recently has received little more than scant mention as a literary curiosity. John Moss, however, in *Patterns of Isolation* (1974), subjects it to an extended analysis both of characters and plot, concluding that

> What sets *Wacousta* apart as something more than a lurid, subliminally obscene, melodrama of revenge are precisely those characteristics which make it the prototype, as previously defined, of one stream in the

flow of Canadian fiction. Exile, in this novel, is a state of mind; the frontier, a state of consciousness. . . . [The] Canadian setting has neither the social complexity nor the sublime, indifferent beauty and order that Frances Brooke perceived in the Canada of her experience. It is, rather, the landscape of a troubled dream; dark, forbidding, filled with murderous savages and murderous intent, a chaotic malevolence streaked with intimations of virtue and stained with the bloodshed of human depravity. It is the outer perimeter of reality, a morass of limitless depth, and man at its centre is in utter isolation, turned in upon himself—his actions and emotions, the self-fulfilling prophecies of his own demise.[13]

Richardson's fondness for the melodramatic, which reflected the taste of his audience, moved easily from fiction into history as an excerpt from *The War of 1812* suggests:

[As an American prisoner sat awaiting his fate,] a young warrior, obeying a signal from one of the elders, rose from his seat, and coming round and behind the prisoner, struck him one blow with his tomahawk on the uncovered head, and he ceased to live. Not a yell, not a sound beside that of the crashing tomahawk was heard, not a muscle of an Indian face was moved. The young warrior, replacing his weapon, walked deliberately back, and resumed his seat in the circle. The whole party remained a few minutes longer seated, and then rose to their feet, and silently withdrew—leaving to those who had not been of the war-party to dispose of the body of the victim. Tecumseh was not present at this scene.[14]

There is much bloodletting in *Wacousta* as well, where the "fancy" has been given even more room for invention and elaboration of scenes like the "brief but terrible scene" describing the killing of Colonel De Haldimar's daughter by Wacousta and the ensuing death of Wacousta himself. As C. F. Klinck says in his introduction to the New Canadian Library edition of *Wacousta*, one of the distinctive features is "the suddenness with which things happen; suspense and shock are practised to the limit."[15] Such technique is evident at the commencement of the passage just referred to:

At about half an hour before midday the air became more rarefied, and the murky clouds, gradually disappearing, left the blue autumnal sky without spot or blemish. Presently, as the bells of the fort struck twelve, a yell as of a legion of devils rent the air, and riveting their gaze in that direction all beheld the bridge, hitherto deserted, suddenly covered with a multitude of savages, among whom were several individuals attired in the European garb and evidently prisoners. Each officer had a telescope raised to his eye, and each prepared himself, shudderingly, for some horrid consummation. . . .[16]

Such a passage illustrates, in addition to Richardson's fondness for melodramatic surprise, his habitual use of the *tableau*-type scene, deliberately enhanced here by the device of the telescopes, one to each officer-viewer. It is hardly too much to say that every time Richardson prepares a scene he does it in terms of romantic painting, just as James Fenimore Cooper, Washington Irving, and others composed their landscapes to resemble, consciously or not, the canvases of the Hudson River school. The conversation is similarly pedestalized, as in this exchange in the midst of some desperate hand-to-hand fighting:

"If François come not we are lost; the howl of that wolf-dog alone will betray us, even if his master should be beyond all chance of recovery."

"Desperate diseases require desperate remedies," was the reply; "there is little glory in destroying a helpless enemy, but the necessity is urgent, and we must leave nothing to chance."[17]

Inevitably, Richardson has been compared with Cooper, not to his advantage, but it needs to be remembered, as Moss's commentary in *Patterns of Isolation* makes clear, that although the two men are dealing with substantially the same set of materials, their separate approaches have quite different purposes. Cooper's frontier, to the man who is strong enough to accept and respond to its positive values (Cooper's fictional treatment of women is notoriously lacking), is viewed as beneficent, not degrading, to Indian and white man alike. Further north, the novelists both early and late are not so sure. When we come to a masterpiece in our own time like Sheila Watson's *The Double Hook* (1959) which tells us unforgettably how rude-spoken, unbending, and bone-wearying frontier life can continue to be, it will not be amiss to recall some of the crudities of early North American settlement and the limited responses that early fiction or other literature of the time was able to give. The pioneers, Puritan and otherwise, lived and died but their unstylish life-style was not so quickly perishable as they were. In *The Double Hook* the people are symbolic, but they are also culturally real.

CHAPTER 2

Haliburton to Moodie

Some of our admirable modern works of fiction, or rather truths disguised in order to render them more palatable to the generality of readers, have done more to ameliorate the sorrows of mankind, by drawing the attention of the public to the wants and woes of the lower classes, than all the charity sermons that have been delivered from the pulpit.

Yes, the despised and reprobated novelists, by daring to unveil the crimes and miseries of neglected and ignorant men, and to point out the abuses which have produced and which are still producing the same dreadful results, are missionaries in the cause of humanity, the real friends and benefactors of mankind.

—S. S. Moodie, *"A Word for the Novel Writers"*

THE principal writers to be met in this chapter, Thomas Chandler Haliburton and Susanna Strickland Moodie, are part of the general advance of fiction in English out of the eighteenth century world of Fielding and Richardson toward the nineteenth century one of Dickens. This was a movement that had no uniform timetable, especially in colonial or lately colonial regions, where undisguised didacticism mingled freely with an increasing concern with character for its own sake. We have seen that Thomas McCulloch was ready to use fiction as a moralist's ploy, and another Scottish writer of the 1820s, in Upper Canada to the west, had purposes similar to McCulloch's. John Galt, working with the Canada Company's colonization project between 1826 and 1829, published in England two novels, *Lawrie Todd* (1830) and *Bogle Corbet* (1831), the product of his Canadian years. The area of their action is the American-Canadian border country of upper New York state, not far from the region where James Fenimore Cooper lived for a time and which he used as setting for the Leather-Stocking Tales. Galt's aim was to create a sympathetic picture of settlement that would foster emigration, especially from Scotland. Parts of *Bogle Corbet* are set in Glasgow, London, and Jamaica before the emigrants reach Canada. One of the characters to emerge was a Yankee named Zerobabel L. Hoskins, the first such to appear in Canadian fiction but not destined for greatness as was Sam Slick. The origin of the "stage Yankee" has been inconclusively debated among folklorists, but it is evident that Haliburton did not invent him. He did, however, significantly mature him and extend his range. Prior to Artemus Ward and Hosea Biglow, Sam had the field pretty much to himself, with only "Major Jack Downing" as fit company.

I *Thomas Chandler Haliburton*

Haliburton, an eminent Nova Scotian whose personality in most particulars would certainly fit the definition of early nineteenth-century Canadian gentility, was attracted also to the ungenteel, the uncouth, as any humorist must be: this is the one element in human nature he can least afford to ignore. Sam Slick, the Yankee supersalesman and raconteur de luxe of Haliburton's *Clockmaker* stories, was the brash counterfoil to many of the values Maritime society had come to cherish; indeed, it had been to escape from political excesses and hatreds that many of their United Empire Loyalist forebears had migrated to Nova Scotia. Most of them could not see, as Haliburton could, that Sam had at least a few ideas worth listening to: that, in fact, is why he came to life, not chiefly to entertain people but to make them think. Fiction, to be acceptable at all, needed to be fitted to such a didactic handle.

As the friend and colleague of Joseph Howe, editor of a Halifax newspaper, the *Nova Scotian*, Haliburton had a ready outlet for the *Clockmaker* sketches as originally written; and in 1836 the first series was gathered into a book, with others to follow. On the formal literary side, the most evident suggestions for narrative structuring—the framework of two men travelling together, one a high-minded intellectual, the other a plainspoken man-of-the-people type—came from a number of eighteenth-century adaptations of *Don Quixote*, the one closest to hand having been *Modern Chivalry* by the Pennsylvania jurist-raconteur H.H. Brackenridge (four parts, between 1792 and 1815). But it was ideas, not episodes, that interested Haliburton, who was also a circuit judge.

Whereas Brackenridge and his British predecessors had been content chiefly with slapstick and caricature, Haliburton had a message to deliver: Nova Scotians (or less elegantly Bluenoses), wake up and join the nineteenth century! His aims, as set forth in retrospect (in the valedictory address prefixed to *The Attaché*, Second Series, 1844), were

. . . to portray character—to give practical lessons in morals, and politics—to expose hypocrisy—to uphold the connection between the parent country and the colonies, to develop the resources of the province and to enforce the just claims of my countrymen—to discountenance agitation—to strengthen the union between Church and State—and to foster and excite a love for our own form of government, and a preference for it over all others.[1]

Thus emerged one of the earliest exchanges in a long-continuing debate between Canadians and their neighbors to the south. At this early time, the emphasis fell quite naturally not upon the United States as an economic and social giant whose influence threatened continually to submerge the Canadian identity, but as an up-and-coming young democracy whose spirit and achievements should be studied and emulated. Haliburton was a born political analyst in an age that produced de Tocqueville; to him, all the way from the Sam Slick sketches to *The Season Ticket* (1860), written about British railway travel, mobility had seemed the key to political survival and growth, particularly in North America where there was still a vast continent to be moved into. Twenty years earlier, in *The Letter Bag of the Great Western; or, Life in a Steamer* (1840) sea travel was the mode emphasized, but the idea was the same, tied up with the reciprocal relations between movement and the power to produce it which was also political power. While Sam Slick, then, was a "cute" Yankee who had a yarn for every household in which he hoped to sell a clock (and usually did), his stories quickly became instances of how-to or how-not-to.

Much has been written about Haliburton's relationship with American humorists, both contemporary (for example, Seba Smith, author of the "Jack Downing" letters which appeared at approximately the same time as *The Clockmaker)* and later James Russell Lowell's Biglow and Charles Farrar Browne's Artemus Ward. Haliburton's purposes most closely resemble those of Lowell, writing during two wars, and of David Ross Locke, author of the Petroleum V. Nasby Letters throughout the American Civil War and into Reconstruction. All three were patriot-humorists who invented characters as vehicles for ideas and programs of action, not merely as entertainers or crackerbox moralists. When Haliburton took up residence in England (where ultimately he became a Member of Parliament) Sam Slick went with him and performed overseas—a different personality in the new surroundings and never so authentic and so popular as the original.

Haliburton produced other books, both before and after *The Clockmaker*, almost to the very end of his life. These included a semiautobiographical volume, *The Old Judge* (1849), his "valedictory to a Nova Scotia he failed to convert to his own way of thinking,"[2] and two very creditable studies of the newly emerging tradition of North American humor to which he had contributed so much: *Traits of American Humour by Native Authors* (1852) and *The Americans at Home; or, Byeways, Backwoods, and Prairies* (1854).

In introducing Sam, Haliburton goes straight to the mark by having his foil-character, the Squire, ask Sam about the secret of his success. Sam explains it by demonstrating how he will sell a clock to Deacon Flint, whose farmhouse they are approaching. Once in the house, the master-salesman begins by praising both the property and its owner; then by degrees he reveals that he has only one clock left which he is reluctant to part with because he thinks one of the neighbors, Mrs. Steel, might want it. But since the Deacon is a trusted friend, he will leave the clock in his care and for his use until he can return and see if Mrs. Steel really does intend to buy it.

> "That," said the Clockmaker, as soon as we were mounted—"that I call *human natur'*. Now that clock is sold for 40 dollars; it cost me just 6 dollars and 50 cents. Mrs. Flint will never let Mrs. Steel have the refusal, nor will the Deacon learn, until I call for the clock, that, having once indulged in the use of a superfluity, how difficult it is to give it up. . . . Of fifteen thousand sold by myself and partners in this Province, twelve thousand were left in this manner, and only ten clocks were ever returned; when we called for them, they invariably bought them. We trust to *soft sawder* to get them into the house, and to *human natur'* that they never come out of it."[3]

Sam's pride in his own expertise, coupled with a good-natured cynicism about the gullibility of his customers, leads us all the way back to the first supersalesman in English literature, the Pardoner of *The Canterbury Tales*, cut from the same bolt.

II   *Susanna Strickland Moodie*

For economic reasons, and sometimes for political as well, emigration to Canada began to increase quite markedly in the 1830s and 40s, as it did also to the United States, Australia, New Zealand, and South Africa. Among those coming to "Upper Canada" were two very talented young married women, the Strickland sisters: Susanna Strickland Moodie and Catherine Parr Traill. Both became writers; Susanna, in fact, had already written a novel—"Spartacus: a Roman Story"—before leaving England. The Moodies lived first near Cobourg, then moved to a more remote backwoods area where they spent several years before settling in Belleville in 1840. Two books by Susanna, published in London in 1852 and 1853—*Roughing It in the Bush* and *Life in the Clearings versus the Bush* (after the move to Belleville)— appeared partly in periodicals as well as in book form, chiefly in the *Literary Garland* (1838-1851). In her two main books, Mrs. Moodie's responses to bush life are presented in two layers: the initial shock of coping with real poverty and hardship among culturally uncongenial neighbors, and the later, somewhat softened distancing by the passage of time.

The sketches that became *Roughing It in the Bush* were not all just personal reminiscence. They were "written by a novelist," as Carl F. Klinck reminds us.

There is no way of telling how much in any given chapter is due to experienced fact and how much to literary artifice. She did not pour out her confessions; she dramatized her vision of herself. [4]

Her best work is social commentary, using character sketches of her neighbors to show how wide a gulf could sometimes exist between European-imported gentility and home-grown democracy. She is occasionally astringent in her comments but seldom indignantly overwrought, and invariably entertaining; the instincts of a professional novelist seem to have guided her pen. And there was the de facto need for income from that pen, at times fairly acute. Her one notable predecessor, Frances Brooke, was never in such straits.

The following passage presents Mrs. Moodies' reactions to the "real" backwoods—the Moodies' new location, a land-grant on Upper Katchawanook Lake.

The prospect from the windows of my sister's log hut was not very prepossessing. The small lake in front, which formed such a pretty object in summer, now looked like an extensive field covered with snow, hemmed in from the rest of the world by a dark belt of sombre pine-woods. The clearing round the house was very small, and only just reclaimed from the wilderness, and the greater part of it covered with piles of brushwood, to be burnt the first dry days of spring.

The charred and blackened stumps on the first few acres that had been cleared during the preceding year were everything but picturesque; and I concluded, as I turned, disgusted, from the prospect before me, that there was very little beauty to be found in the backwoods. But I came to this decision during a Canadian thaw, be it remembered, when one is wont to view every object with jaundiced eyes.[5]

The sister, Catherine Parr Traill, was temperamentally a naturalist rather than an observer of human behavior, as a brief passage from *The Backwoods of Canada* (1836) plainly shows:

For myself, though I can easily enter into the feelings of the poet and enthusiastic lover of the wild and the wonderful of historic lore, I can yet make myself very happy and contented in this country. If its volume of history is yet a blank, that of Nature is open, and eloquently marked by the finger of God; and from its pages I can extract a thousand sources of amusement and interest whenever I take my walks in the forest or by the borders of the lakes.[6]

One more excerpt from *Roughing It in the Bush*, developing the kind of personal encounter repeated many times, with variations, presents Susanna fencing verbally with a "borrowing neighbor" who has just sold her a rooster and now wants to borrow some tea.

"My name is Betty Fye—old Betty Fye; I live in the log shanty over the creek, at the back of you'rn. The farm belongs to my eldest son. I'm a widow with twelve sons; and 'tis—hard to scratch along."

"Do you swear?"

"Swear! What harm? It eases one's mind when one's vexed. Everybody swears in this country. My boys all swear like Sam Hill; and I used to swear mighty big oaths till about a month ago, when the Methody parson told me that if I did not leave it off I should go to a tarnation bad place; so I dropped some of the worst of them."

"You would do wisely to drop the rest; women never swear in my country."

"Well, you don't say! I always heer'd they were very ignorant. Will you lend me the tea?"

The woman was such an original that I gave her what she wanted.[7]

Wilfred Eggleston, after quoting Mrs. Moodie on the positive hostility of many frontier women to the "sin of authorship" as they viewed it, observes:

It is, of course, possible that Mrs. Moodie misinterpreted some of these incidents. At the root of the hostility of the pioneer native North American women may have been a natural resentment at Mrs. Moodie's assumption of social superiority. The pioneer women may have secretly envied her talent and experience; and their derogatory remarks about such idle accomplishments as authorship may not have stemmed from active animosity toward writing as such. But the salvation of the pioneer lay . . . in other more practical and non-literary achievements.[8]

That this attitude did not disappear with the coming of the twentieth century is evident in Robert Stead's *Grain* (1926), which relates the following conversation between the central figure, Gander Stake, and his sister:

"Do you know the difference between a noun and a pronoun?" she demanded of her brother one evening at the supper table.

"Don' know as I do," Gander admitted, without apologies.

"Huh. Teacher'd call you a dunce."

"Would she?" said Gander. "Well, I know the difference between a Deering and a Massey-Harris across a fifty-acre field, an' I bet she don't an' you can tell her that for me."[9]

It is no wonder that, a few years later, "growing wheat became a patriotic duty into which Gander fitted like a cylinder nut into a socket wrench."[10]

CHAPTER 3

Kirby to Leacock

There is an excellent tradition in our culture of letters. One of the great cultural vehicles of early Canadian society is letters, and it comes through a tradition which of course we've rejected as being non-Canadian, and that is the genteel tradition, the tradition of the British Upper Class in Canada. We've rejected that because it seems unCanadian, but the fact is that for fifty years at the beginning of the 19th century, this tradition of letters, of which Mrs. Moodie is an excellent example, this tradition was the vehicle for something fine in being Canadian and it helped me write. . . . We still have this vestige of British civility. . . . of gentility, even though god knows we're systematically destroying it, because it bothers those that ain't got it, and those who've got it tend to use it badly as a snobbery. So there's that advantage of vestigial gentility.

—Scott Symons

CANADIAN Confederation—the achievement of Dominion status, in 1867—produced a sizable tide of patriotic sentiment lasting for several decades, but it did not perfectly unite the country and quiet her political dissent. Only two years later occurred the first of two armed rebellions in the Canadian Midwest, led by Louis Riel, who resisted transfer of the Hudson's Bay Company's territorial rights to the Canadian government, and throughout the 1870s remained a stormy figure in frontier politics. After a second uprising in 1884–85 Riel was captured and, amid a great emotional upheaval, hanged for treason. These events brought out rather more of a poetic than a fictional response (Riel himself was a poet, in French), but one novel related to the first rebellion, *Dot-It-Down* (1871) by Alexander Begg, looks satirically at the Riel partisans. A hundred years later, as we shall see, Riel had become a folk hero and Canadian contemporaries were turning to these events not only in fiction but in all literary genres.

I   *William Kirby*

Not unnaturally, historically-minded Canadians of the 1870s looked back for at least a century and at times two. For tastes still under the sway of Sir Walter Scott, assisted by a number of semiliterary historians, the French regime in early Quebec seemed the proper distance for romantic fiction, especially when "novel" and "romance" were not yet easily distinguishable. Add to this a growing proclivity to melodrama, and the time is ripe for such a novel as *The Golden Dog* (1877) by William Kirby, who had begun the work in 1865 and "worked long . . . to stir his fellow countrymen with a sense of their past."[1]

The Golden Dog, the only work for which Kirby is remembered, was acceptable at the time of its publication not so much because it took a new direction (others had written reams about "Old Quebec") but because it was a handling of French culture by an English-bred writer whose knowledge of history and manners was both deep and sympathetic. It is set in Quebec, in the year 1748, and well-laced with French phrases, verses of songs, and other rhymes. The plot swirls about two women, Angelique de Meloises who unscrupulously attempts to gain power through marriage, and her virtuous counterfoil Amelie de Repentigny who is destroyed by Angelique's machinations. Of local color, a passage such as this one is representative:

The gay chorus of the voyageurs made the shores ring, as they kept time with their oars, while the silver spray dripped like a shower of diamonds in the bright sunshine at every stroke of their rapid paddles.[2]

and as examples of the other side, involving poison, daggers, murders, inflated speeches—all the consequences of ambitious love:

Happy had it been for her never to have opened that fatal door.[3]

or:

The angel of death had kissed her lovingly, and unnoticed of any she had passed with him away![4]

A predecessor of Kirby's in the use of French-Canadian subjects was Rosanna Leprohon (1829-1879), who contributed to the

Literary Garland and other periodicals, and in three novels—*Le Manoir de Villerai* (1859), *Antoinette de Mirecourt* (1864), and *Armand Durand* (1868)—"became one of the first Canadian writers in English to explore in detail French-Canadian subjects and to have works on these subjects translated into French and widely praised by French Canadians."[5] Kirby had very little other book-length precedent for his work, although there had been in the 1870s a fair bit of short fiction (and some serialized novels) in magazines. Statistics cited by Gordon Roper are most revealing on this point: up to 1880, some 150 authors had published little more than 250 volumes, whereas during the years 1880 to 1920 (approximately the limits of this chapter) more than four hundred authors had appeared, publishing over fourteen hundred volumes. "Charles G. D. Roberts, Gilbert Parker, Robert Barr, James Oxley, Theodore Roberts, and Margaret Marshall Saunders together accounted for more than 200 of this total, and fifteen other writers published from nine to twenty volumes each."[6] In Canada, and in the United States of Mark Twain and W. D. Howells, authorship was comparatively more lucrative in the later nineteenth century than it is today. The American market, magazine-writing and book-publishing alike, was open to Canadians, some of whom became long-term residents of the United States.

II *James De Mille*

A failed bookseller turned college professor (principally at Dalhousie University from 1864 until his death), James De Mille was one of the writers who set about systematically to supplement his income by writing what would sell. For Harper & Brothers, his chief publishers, he averaged better than a book a year for two decades—a series for boys (a "Brethren of the White Cross" sequence), historical romances, mystery stories and melodramas, together with two novels, *The Dodge Club; or, Italy in 1859* (1867) and *A Strange Manuscript Found in a Copper Cylinder* (posthumously published, 1888). The first of these novels uses North American travellers abroad as the objects of its humor, in addition to undertaking "a clever parody upon the melodramatic novel in which De Mille was so proficient."[7]

The *Strange Manuscript,* on the other hand, goes well beyond parody into satiric utopianism, its date of composition falling close to Samuel Butler's *Erewhon* (1872) which in its social topsy-turviness it resembles (although reversals and inversions are common devices in much satire of this type). George Woodcock calls it a "solitary masterpiece"—"the first utopian romance written by a Canadian, and almost the last"—a "well-written and boldly speculative book, in quite another category from most of the banal adventure narratives which Canadian writers were publishing copiously at the time."[8] In itself the book is still a mystery; scholarly research has not yet answered many questions about De Mille and his long-unpublished masterpiece. Did he submit it for publication and have it refused? Did he leave, at his early death (presumably unexpected), any provision for his literary estate? How *did* the manuscript at length reach *Harper's Weekly* and eventually book publication? Seeing that it appeared in the same year as Edward Bellamy's *Looking Backward* we may surmise that it was chosen because the climate was right for even an anti-utopian romance, a *Looking Downward* so to speak, but that is still only a surmise. One book alongside a middling lot of others hardly makes a major writer, but it is still true that *A Strange Manuscript* is the finest piece of Canadian fiction before 1890 (the year Sara Jeannette Duncan began publishing), and we need to know more about its author and its own strange manuscript story.

This book has a multidimensional structure quite uncommon for the time of its composition, the 1870s. First of all, the author provides a narrative abounding in marvels, mystery, and semi-horror for the first half dozen chapters, involving the reader deeply in the predicament of his hero, Adam More, before beginning to develop the "Kosekin" philosophy of self-abasement, poverty, and death which is found in an extensive civilization at the South Pole. Allowing these repellent ideas to percolate slowly into Adam's mind, the author interrupts the narrative periodically by reverting to the discovery-framework, a British nobleman's leisurely cruising yacht upon which an assorted quartet engage in speculation and lively debate about the manuscript's content and authenticity. Just when we are beginning to think that Adam More (now "Atam-or" in the new language he must learn) is doing nicely with his newfound sweetheart Almah, another beauty enters the picture to complicate matters and, concomitantly, to supply ironic amusement. At times De Mille seems to be well outside his own work, looking back at it and poking fun, at other times seriously musing about the human condition, but never overtly grinding any personal or institutional axe. The technique in places is Conradian (the yacht scenes especially) years before Joseph Conrad; Huxleyian and Orwellian decades before Aldous Huxley and George Orwell.

Briefly to describe the central ideology of the work, instead of celebrating life the Kosekins despise it, regarding death as its sole aim and greatest benefit. (Why then be born?—so that we may enjoy the bliss of death.) Not unexpectedly, they are regarded by their involuntary visitors as "a nation of kind-hearted and amiable miscreants—of generous, refined, and most self-denying fiends; of men who were highly civilized, yet utterly wrong-headed and irreclaimable in their bloodthirsty cruelty."[9] Paupers, revolting in appearance and arrogantly self-righteous in manner, thorough-paced latter-day Struldbrugs, are the leading citizens and policy-makers. One of the priests, still aspiring to pauperdom (not easily achieved, because of fierce competition for the distinction it confers), explains:

"We are so made that we cannot help loving death; it is a sort of instinct. We are also created in such a way that we cannot help longing after poverty. The pauper must always, among all men, be the most envied of mortals. Nature, too, has made us such that the passion of love, when it arises, is so vehement, so all-consuming that it must always struggle to avoid requital. This is the reason why, when two people find that they love each other, they always separate and avoid one another for the rest of their lives. This is human nature. We cannot help it; and it is this that distinguishes us from the animals. Why, if men were to feel as you say you feel, they would be mere animals. Animals fear death; animals love to accumulate such things as they prize; animals, when they love, go in pairs, and remain with one another. But man, with his intellect, would not be man if he loved life and desired riches and sought for requited love."[10]

This is only in confirmation of what Almah has told her lover at the outset:

Almah shook her head. "You do not understand these people," said she. "Their ruling passion is the hatred of self, and therefore they are eager to confer benefits on others. The only hope of life that I have for you and for myself is in this, that if they kill us they will lose their most agreeable occupation. They value us most highly, because we take everything that is given us. You and I now possess as our own property all this city and all its buildings, and all the people have made themselves our slaves."[11]

The opposition minority, which De Mille is careful to provide as prompting the reader to interior dialogue of his own, is also allowed to speak:

> I soon learned that the Kohen Gadol was what we term "a man of advanced views," or perhaps a "Reformer," or a "Philosophic Radical," it matters not which; suffice it to say that his ideas and feelings differed from those of his nation, and if carried out would be equal to a revolution in politics and morals.
>
> The Kohen Gadol advocated selfishness as the true law of life, without which no state can prosper. There were a few of similar views, but they were all regarded with great contempt by the multitude, and had to suffer the utmost rigor of the law; for they were all endowed with vast wealth, compelled to live in the utmost splendor and luxury, to have enormous retinues, and to wield the chief power in politics and in religion. Even this, however, had not changed the sentiments of the condemned, and I learned that they were laboring incessantly, notwithstanding their severe punishment, to disseminate their peculiar doctrines. These were formulated as follows:
>
> 1 A man should not love others better than himself.
> 2 Life is an evil to be got rid of.
> 3 Other things are to be preferred to death.
> 4 Poverty is not the best state for man.
> 5 Unrequited love is not the greatest happiness.
> 6 Lovers may sometimes marry.
> 7 To serve is not more honorable than to command.
> 8 Defeat is not more glorious than victory.
> 9 To save a life should not be regarded as a criminal offence.
> 10 The paupers should be forced to take a certain amount of wealth, to relieve the necessities of the rich.[12]

The numerology here, together with much of the content, is hardly a mere accident; we have the "natural" reaction to a kind of inverted Ten Commandments, such as Orwell's "War Is Peace," "Ignorance Is Strength," etc. The Kosekins, however, are not consistently anti-Christian. They would for instance endorse such sentiments as "sell all you have and give to the poor" or "he that loseth his life shall save it." Theirs too is a species of "divine madness," perverse as it may be, and the learned author of *A Strange Manuscript*, probing gently but nevertheless painfully, does not neglect to point out that Buddha, Sophocles, and others held views not radically different. To succeed as satire, it all must carry the gloss of possibility, if not necessarily plausibility, and it does so.

Perhaps if one could decant Butler's *Erewhon* (1872) along with Swinburne's "The Garden of Proserpine" (1866) into a copper cylinder as cocktail-shaker, the emergent mixture might taste a little like De Mille's philosophico-elegiac, satirico-romantic shandy.

III   Sara Jeannette Duncan

Between Susanna Moodie and Sara Jeannette Duncan, whose first novel appeared in 1890, there was no lack of Canadian women novelists. None rose to first rank, but some of them wrote voluminously—May Agnes Fleming, for instance, who kept Street & Smith's *New York Weekly* supplied with society romances offered as counterweights to Wild West stories by Ned Buntline and other dime novelists; Mary Anne Sadlier and Anna Teresa Sadlier, a mother-daughter team; and Agnes Maule Machar, one of the mainstays of the *Canadian Monthly*. All of them, each according to her own abilities, were professional authors.

Sara Jeannette Duncan, who has sometimes been called the "Canadian Jane Austen," is rather more like George Eliot in her highly developed ability to handle ideas along with describing human behavior. In her twenties she gravitated naturally to journalism, working for such distinguished newspapers as the Toronto *Globe* and the Washington *Post*. Soon she was travelling and beginning to experience the exhilarations of living abroad with which Henry James endows several of his heroines. Her first novel appeared in London in 1890, under the breezy title *A Social Departure: How Orthodicia and I Went Round the World by Ourselves*. But she did not return alone, or at least very long remain so, for having met a young man in India, she became Mrs. Everard C. Cotes in 1891 and took up residence there; her husband was Curator of the Indian Museum, Calcutta. Although this circumstance changed the direction of her career considerably, she did not leave the theme of the young woman abroad until she had published *An American Girl in London* (1891), *Those Delightful Americans* (1902—the girl this time is English, coming west), and *Cousin Cinderella: a Canadian Girl in London* (1908). The following brisk exchange from *An American Girl in London* involves Mamie Wick, from Chicago, who has been asked by her "poppa" to call on his London aunt, a Mrs. Portheris. Mamie is received with "armed neutrality" and no little surprise that her mother and father are not along.

"Then I suppose," said Mrs. Portheris—the supposition being of the vaguest possible importance—"that you are with a party of Americans. It seems to be an American idea to go about in hordes. I never could understand it—to me it would be most obnoxious. How many are there of you?"

"One, Mrs. Portheris—and I'm the one. Poppa and momma had set their hearts on coming. Poppa thought of getting up an Anglo-American Soda Trust, and momma wanted particularly to make your acquaintance—your various Christmas cards have given us all such a charming idea of you—but at the last minute something interfered with their plans and they had to give it up. They told me to tell you how sorry they were."

"Something interfered with their plans! But nothing interfered with *your* plans!"

"Oh, no; it was some political business of poppa's—nothing to keep me!"

"Then do I actually understand that your parents, of their *own free will*, permitted you to cross the Atlantic *alone*?"

"I hope you do, Mrs. Portheris; but if it's not quite clear to you, I don't mind explaining it again."

"Upon my word! And you are at an hotel—which hotel?"

When I told Mrs. Portheris the Metropole, her indignation mounted to her cap, and one of the pink ribbons shook violently.

"It is very American!" she said; and I felt that Mrs. Portheris could rise to no more forcible a climax of disapproval.[13]

In her Indian group of six novels, Sara Duncan began with *The Simple Adventures of a Memsahib* (1893) and *Vernon's Aunt: Being the Oriental Experiences of Miss Lavinia Moffat* (1894), both "initiation" or "transition" stories. Then in four later volumes—*His Honour and a Lady* (1896), *The Path of a Star* (1899), *Set in Authority* (1908), and *The Burnt Offering* (1909)—she undertook more complex social and political issues, fully aware of the violence already smoldering in India before Gandhi.

In the face of all this, had she forgotten her Canadian origins? With a new subcontinent around her she well might have; but she had not; and in *The Imperialist* (1904)—which appeared midway between *A Daughter of Today* (1894—chronicling a "New Woman" of a century ago) and *The Consort* (1912) and *His Royal Happiness* (1914), all political novels in the broad sense of dealing with power and the search for power—she published her best-remembered book. She liked to think of Canada as a rational compromise between British conservatism and American excess, having experienced all three societies in the Atlantic triangle. She recalled, too, in *The Imperialist,* her first love, the world of journalism, reexplored through the personalities of editors and the policies of their papers in provincial Ontario. Writing with absolute confidence in the knowledge of her material, she interpolates the occasional sharp chapter of analytical comment (Chapter 7 is a good example) besides handling two romances, both provided with abundant obstacles and offering surprises at the end. She uses dances and dinner parties as narrative-descriptive opportunities, somewhat in the manner of James and Howells (both of whom she admired), and through the numerous young women and their parents evokes a strong sense of family life. Portraits of Dr. Drummond, the senior local clergyman (Presbyterian) and his very different young colleague, Hugh Finlay from Scotland, are well drawn. The hero, Lorne Murchison, loses both his election and his fiancée, but is still on his feet at the end. The "imperialism" he stood for looks, almost a century later than the supposed time of action, much like the loosely federated cooperation of today's Commonwealth, with Canada a full partner— argued for, then, as a check to the threat of only too genuine economic imperialism from the United States. The issues raised are by no means dead ones yet; students of government, in addition to readers who simply enjoy good writing, would find much in *The Imperialist* to interest them, such as this specimen of political oratory by the young candidate, Lorne Murchison, from whose views the novel takes its title:

"It is ours," he told them, "in this greater half of the continent, to evolve a nobler ideal. The Americans from the beginning went in a spirit of revolt; the seed of disaffection was in every Puritan bosom. We from the beginning went in a spirit of amity, forgetting nothing, disavowing nothing, to plant the flag with our fortunes. We took our very Constitution, our very chart of national life, from England—her laws, her liberty, her equity were good enough for us. We have lived by them, some of us have died by them . . . and, thank God, we were long poor. . . .

"And this Republic," he went on hotly, "this Republic that menaces our national life with commercial extinction, what past has she that is comparable? The daughter who left the old stock to be the light woman among nations, welcoming all comers, polluting her lofty ideals until it is hard indeed to recognize the features and the aims of her honourable youth. . . ."

Allowance will be made for the intemperance of his figure. He believed himself, you see, at the bar for the life of a nation.

". . . Let us not hesitate to announce ourselves for the Empire, to throw all we are and all we have into the balance for that great decision. The seers of political economy tell us that if the stars continue to be propitious, it is certain that a day will come which will usher in a union of the Anglo-Saxon nations of the world. As between England and the United States the predominant partner in that firm will be one that brings Canada. So that the imperial movement of the hour may reach even farther than the boundaries of Great Britain. . . ."[14]

IV   Fiction for an Expanding Readership; Best Sellers

The figures for novels appearing in 1880–1920, quoted earlier in this chapter, indicate that the 1890s were a major watershed for Canadian authorship. A North American population that had been increasing at astonishing rates from one census to the next, since the end of the American Civil War, was also becoming literate far more rapidly than at any other time in human history; moreover, it was becoming far more mobile and reaping the cultural advantages of mobility. Hunger for print, in consequence—for stories of new places dwelt in by strange people or even ingratiatingly familiar ones—became curiously strong in the later nineteenth century and, in relative terms, could be easily, quickly, cheaply satisfied. Haliburton, in the 1830s, wrote for his neighbors and chanced upon a wider readership; in another fifty or sixty years, it was well understood that no writer need be confined by local limitations, for a truly vast audience was ready and waiting if only one had the wit to sense what was most wanted. And while public taste was not always accurately predictable or uniformly high (when was it ever?), there was room for a good bit of variety.

Gilbert Parker, like Haliburton, completed his career in England, where he was knighted in 1902 and served variously as a member of Parliament, member of the Privy Council, and propaganda chief for North America during World War I. In the midst of all this he remained one of the most prolific of all Canadian novelists, averaging about a book a year from the publication of his first stories, *Pierre and His People*, in 1892, until his death. Early studies in theology and the teaching of elocution (in Canada) produced in his work a strong bent toward melodrama and romantically heightened rhetoric. His critics were not slow to point out these weaknesses, but were obliged to concede that he was able to build himself into an impressive public figure as well as a highly visible man of letters.

Parker, like Kirby before him, responded emotionally to French-Canadian history and used French Canada as the scene of about a fourth of his novels (partially collected, 1912–23, in a sumptuous Imperial Edition of twenty-three volumes; his total output includes at least a dozen more). Among these, *When Valmond Came to Pontiac* (1895) and *The Seats of the Mighty* (1896) have weathered best. The Canadian Northwest was another locale he favored, as in *Northern Lights* (1895) and other volumes appearing ten to fifteen years later. This comment on the north, put into the mouth of Pierre in Parker's first book, is a good sample of the style and mood he cultivated in his later fiction:

> Pierre began: "You have seen it beautiful and cold in the north, but never so cold and beautiful as it was last year. The world was white with sun and ice, the frost never melting, the sun never warming—just a glitter, so lovely, so deadly. If only you could keep the heart warm, you were not afraid. But if once—just for a moment—the blood ran out from the heart and did not come in again, the frost clamped the doors shut, and there was an end of all. Ah, m'sieu', when the north clinches a man's heart in anger there is no pain like it—for a moment."[15]

Having already written an early journalistic account of Australia, following a trip to the South Seas in 1891, Parker came finally to use scattered parts of the British Empire as settings for novels. Today he is largely a forgotten giant, or one who at the time looked like a giant. "Perhaps," says a recent estimate, "he was most just to himself when he wrote 'I was a born dramatist.' For, in spite of his aggrandizement of his work, he was a successful writer of fiction of strong effect. His strength lay in his power of creating spirited action, and enhancing it with romantic atmosphere."[16] No one can deny that this is a formula or a recipe still very much in vogue, and Parker was one of the first Canadians to have used it in the grand manner throughout a long career.

Two other expatriate writers of this era (observe how many native or adopted Canadians during the expansionist period of Canadian writing found it necessary or convenient to live and work outside the country) were rather more novelists of ideas, like Sara Jeannette Duncan, than romancers: Grant Allen and Robert Barr. Allen wrote chiefly upon science and its meaning for society, but employed fiction at times to advance his views, as in the anti-utopian *Philistia* (1884) and *The Woman Who Did* (1895), a defense of sexual freedom. Barr was likewise a satirist and social critic, of American and Canadian public affairs; his comment in the *Canadian Magazine* for November 1899 expresses succinctly what he thought of the literary scene: "The bald truth is that Canada has the money, but would rather spend it on whiskey than on books."

Both Allen and Barr found London the best base of operations. Not so another Ontario writer, the Reverend Charles W. Gordon who at the end of the 1890s burst upon the publishing scene as an unheralded best-selling novelist. "Ralph Connor," the name under which Gordon wrote, wished to demonstrate through his heroes the positive values of religious life, especially in pioneering or semipioneering rural communities. In one of his best-known stories (he wrote some thirty books in all, between 1898 and 1936), *The Man from Glengarry* (1901), Ranald Macdonald grows to manhood with high moral standards as the result of his friendship with the local minister's wife, Mrs. Murray. Frontier life in Glengarry, the most easterly Ontario country, is described as lived in the 1860s: sugaring, logging, rowdy fights, and loyal friendships are the experiences of a cross-section of Scottish, French Canadian, and Irish characters. Following is a passage in which the author emphasizes the overmastering quality of the forest in the farthest reaches of settlement: after "some dozen or more of the crossroads marking the concessions which lead off to east and west have been passed, the road seems to strike into a different world."

The forest loses its conquered appearance, and dominates everything. There is forest everywhere. It lines up close and thick along the road, and here and there quite overshadows it. It crowds in upon the little farms and shuts them off from one another and from the world outside, and peers in through the little windows of the log houses looking so small and lonely, but so beautiful in their forest frames.[17]

Nor is this merely fanciful landscape. "In the local-colour tradition too," says Ross Beharriell, "the fictional background of the book is meticulously faithful to the original Glengarry landscape. From the carefully co-ordinated descriptions of the forests, the brûlés, the farms, the streams, one can readily picture the area;

and the imaginative reconstruction corresponds in every detail to the original."[18]

Connor's success of seventy years ago is well matched by that of Lucy Maud Montgomery in *Anne of Green Gables* (1908) and succeeding "Anne" books. So many Canadian (and other) novelists today assert, and in their stories demonstrate, that childhood is the period during which one is culturally stunted and/or, at best, receives all sorts of psychological blocks and barriers, that the older views—sternly rejected—tend to drop entirely out of sight. Nowhere were they more alive and well than in Montgomery's books. It would be unrealistic to deny that optimism—after two world wars bracketing a severe economic depression, all with numerous violent side-effects—may be wearing a trifle thin, and that childhood a generation later, for one reason or another, often does have serious problems unheard of, even undreamed of, before 1910. Granting this, some light on fictional responses to life in two widely spaced generations may be gained from a comparison between *Anne of Green Gables* and a recent novel about childhood in Montreal during the Depression, Mary Peate's *Girl in a Red River Coat* (1970).

Anne enters the world of Green Gables as unwanted and resented—an orphan. Life deals unkindly enough with her at times, but after a chronicle of mingled disappointments and successes (the latter especially at school), she can agree at the end that "God's in his heaven—All's right with the world," adding on her own, "Dear old world, you are very lovely, and I am glad to be alive in you." No doubt the author's own childhood on Prince Edward Island gave her book the kind of setting in which Anne could win and ultimately thrive. No doubt too, as Marjorie McDowell says, "Defects of sentimentality and over-optimism pass unnoticed in the powerful unity of mood, an outcome of the author's personal and artistic sincerity."[19] Sixty years later Mary, the girl in the Red River coat, is presented as living in a bilingual city, attending parochial school during the Depression (and far from being first in her class, having trouble with her teachers), seeing her world as a maze of streets with men begging meals at the door to her home and the nearby grocery manager committing suicide, disliking a divorced aunt living temporarily with the family because she takes Mary's room, and so forth. At the end, when the aunt leaves, Mary's father quotes—semisardonically—

Browning's lines. "I grinned in agreement, and he continued down the hall" (final sentence).[20] *Girl in a Red River Coat* is certainly not intended as a parody on *Anne of Green Gables*, but in some respects it might almost be taken as such.

V   *Regional Writing, East and West*

In the later nineteenth century, local-color and regional fiction, particularly short stories, enjoyed widespread vogue. Depending on how one defines his terms, some of the popular fiction we have just been briefly surveying might also be called regional even though the writers were eclectic in their choice of settings from one book to another—Parker, for example. At least the diversities of Canadian experience were being further explored; and although apart from the Maritimes there were still no well-defined centers of literary expression, the far West was being looked at by romancers and realists alike. To illustrate an emerging contrast between both physical setting and social scene as between far eastern and far western Canada, the work of two writers, Edward William Thomson and M.A. Grainger, has been selected.

Thomson's *Old Man Savarin Stories; Tales of Canada and Canadians*, recently republished (1974) in a handsome reprint by the University of Toronto Press, appeared in 1917, when Canada was in the midst of World War I and Thomson, after a long career as writer and editor, was himself an old man. The book demonstrates how the author was able to adapt his work to the expanded range and methods of the short story since the original appearance in 1895 of *Old Man Savarin and Other Stories*. Warfare is a theme in several of the 1917 stories, but it is the American Civil War or the Boer War that provides the background. One story, "Boss of the World," treats humorously the dilemma facing the inventor of an Ultimate Weapon (the time is 1915), who is uncertain of finding a nation "animated by liberalism and dominated by conscience" to which it would be safe to entrust his awesome invention. In another thirty years, the question would no longer seem either fantastic or humorous. The change in title underlines, as Thomson's editor Linda Shesko points out, Thomson's "increasing awareness of his role as interpreter of Canadians and Americans to each other."[21] But in 1895, eastern Canada was the focus and Old Man Savarin the central figure in a collection dominated by humor and pathos with narration in French Canadian *patois*. There is every assumption of continuity, of somnolent stability, of the mellowing of a tradition of which Savarin is the product.

M.A. Grainger's *Woodsmen of the West*, published in London in 1908 and illustrated with photographs, is a kind of seminovel, mainly autobiographical with side-skeins of other narrative. Beginning with a logger's-eye view of Vancouver, the story moves quickly to Hanson Island and Carter's Camp, with stories about small steamboats and their troubles and others about grim accidents: drownings, rock-slides, snapped cables, and the like. The manner is direct and forceful, both in description and dialogue. The principal conflict-line is between the narrator and the logging boss Carter, whom he admires for his "romantic battling with work, with nature, and with the hostility of his fellow-man" along with his "ascetic lack of compromise."[22] Several chapters are given to Carter's story. Finally, the narrator is unable to stand Carter's driving manners any longer:

Work was, for him, a vicious habit, and he seethed with anger all through each day to think how purposeless work had become. Times were too bad! Logs were unsaleable! To work and haul logs into water was to let the sea-worms spoil the good wood! Not to work was to go through nervous torture![23]

At the end he says

Farewell, then, to wrenching and tearing and intensity of effort; to great fatigues and physical discomforts; to sweaty work with simple tools; to trails in far-away mountain places; to rest and warmth beside log-fires in the woods![24]

Woodsmen of the West, by consensus of three critics in *The Literary History of Canada*, is "one of the finest pieces of local and psychological realism in Canadian writing."[25]

These two works are at the geographical extremes of east and west, and there are others of about the same time which relate to still other localities. Charles G. D. Roberts and Duncan Campbell Scott, from the Maritimes, were two of the leading figures at the turn of the century and later, writing both poetry and short fiction. From Ontario came Stephen Leacock, the next writer to be considered.

VI   *Stephen Leacock*

Having just encountered a talent as good as Sara Jeannette
Duncan's we can see plainly enough that Canada did not lack
potential for humorous writing. The market was another matter.
For example, Norah Story tells us that in 1906, "John Francis
Wilson looked for a publisher for *The Migration of Skivens*, a
comic presentation of his experiences on arrival in Manitoba in
1888, but no publisher would accept this amusingly written and
illustrated book and it was not published until 1962."[26] In 1906,
notwithstanding, Robert Barr had published a satire on public
education in Ontario, *The Measure of the Rule*, and Duncan's
work was becoming well known. Local-color writing not infre-
quently employed humor of a rather mild sort, including humorous dialect. When, therefore, in 1910 a professor of economics
from McGill University named Stephen Leacock published his
first volume of sketches called *Literary Lapses*, readers in Canada—and even more to the point, in the English-speaking world
outside—were ready for a humorous writer of his temperament
and staying power.

Apparently Leacock was himself unaware that the world was
waiting for him; *Literary Lapses* was printed at his own expense
and sold for thirty-five cents—surely not a deliberate gambit by
an expert in economics. Thus one of his first jokes was on himself,
pleasantly enough. Most of the pieces in *Literary Lapses* had been
published in magazines, but the author had at the time no dream
of the literary career immediately ahead of him. His topics were
those that interested, and still interest, us all: food, money,
schooling, courtship and marriage, doctors, barbers, and parlor
pastimes (to while away the Canadian winter), mingled with
burlesques of popular poetry and fiction.

But Leacock had more than merely a shrewd sense of what an
audience might like, important as that always is to the practicing
humorist. From somewhere he had received the gift of objectify-
ing and personalizing abstractions, and of taking metaphors
literally—the humorist's pose of the inspired idiot. For instance,
he quotes a problem in arithmetic: "A, B, and C do a certain piece
of work. A can do as much work in one hour as B in two, or C in
four. Find out how long they work at it."[27] After Leacock finishes
introducing "the human element in mathematics" A, B, and C
have become actual people and the "certain piece of work" is

similarly alive. "A Lesson in Fiction" deals with clichés of plot and character in such a way as to point strongly toward *Nonsense Novels* (1911), the book immediately following. For example, one of the most oft-quoted sentences in all of Leacock (and there is a great deal)—"Lord Ronald said nothing; he flung himself from the room, flung himself upon his horse and rode madly off in all directions" ("Gertrude the Governess, or Simple Seventeen")[28]—is borrowed out of "A Lesson in Fiction": "De Vaux sank from his hoo-doo on to the sands, while the affrighted elephant dashed off in all directions."[29]

There are many fine things in *Nonsense Novels*, inviting us to read madly off in all directions, but a couple of more samples must here suffice. The first describes Isolde the Slender, heroine of *Guido the Gimlet of Ghent;* the second is by the narrator of *Soaked in Seaweed, or Upset in the Ocean.*

Willowy and slender in form, she was as graceful as a meridian of longitude. Her body seemed almost too frail for motion, while her features were of a mould so delicate as to preclude all thought of intellectual operation.[30]

I stood there leaning over the gaff of the mainsail and thinking—yea, thinking, dear reader, of my mother. I hope you will think none the less of me for that. Whenever things look dark, I lean up against something and think of Mother. If they get positively black, I stand on one leg and think of Father. After that I can face anything.[31]

Of the first two books, *Literary Lapses* can be read longer without seeming to pall, but after over half a century both still retain a large part of their fun, as only a very few humorous works are ever able to do.

Whereas the books described so far are collections of separate pieces, the next contains character studies within a unifying locale which bring it closer to fiction *per se. Sunshine Sketches of a Little Town* (1912), one of the earliest in a long line of what North American critics have come to call "the attack on the village," celebrates without rancor (or at least without very much) the town of "Mariposa," identifiable as Orillia, Ontario, somewhat as a few years later Sinclair Lewis's "Gopher Prairie" of *Main Street* was identifiable as Sauk Center, Minnesota. Mariposa is revealed as overestimating itself, "proud of the trains, even if they don't stop," going for lake (really shallow puddle) excursions on the

"Mariposa Belle," practicing middle-class thrift but ready to speculate on mining shares, listening to Dean Drone's Church of England sermons (there is a clergyman named Dr. Drone in McCulloch's *Stepsure Letters*), sending its sons to die for the Empire in South Africa, heating up at election time, drowsing in the sunshine between such sensations. The final sketch, "The Train to Mariposa," is rather palpably nostalgic. The contemporary novelist Hugh Hood, calling *Sunshine Sketches* "one of the two or three books at the nerve-centre of Canadian life," goes on to say:

> *Sunshine Sketches* is about as Canadian as you can get. Its author was born in England and came here as a baby; his two masters were an English writer and an American: Dickens and Mark Twain. His choice of subject matter and form are, or were, essentially Canadian. The book is a pastoral idyll treated satirically, one of the major literary kinds, perhaps the most appropriate choice of genre in the earlier stages of our history. Nowadays what is wanted is an epic—this is clear enough—with comic interludes but no satiric ones. The heads of our novelists and poets, Murray Sansfoy, Alcide Beaulieu, turn again and again towards Louis Riel, Brebeuf, Almighty Voice, when they might better take a good look at the figure of the locomotive engineer.[32]

With *Sunshine Sketches* Leacock completed establishing himself as a Canadian humorist in addition to having, already, introduced himself into international company. From that point onward, the stage was his whenever he chose to perform. Born into the world of Mark Twain's early successes, he published his own first book in the year of Twain's death. At his own death he was well into the world of James Thurber, and still a stout practitioner of one of the most precarious of all literary arts. He appears to have sensed his mission fairly early, judging from this passage in the preface to *Sunshine Sketches:*

> Many of my friends are under the impression that I write these humorous nothings in idle moments when the wearied brain is unable to perform the serious labours of the economist. My own experience is exactly the other way. The writing of solid, instructive stuff fortified by facts and figures is easy enough. There is no trouble in writing a scientific treatise on the folk-lore of Central China, or a statistical enquiry into the declining population of Prince Edward Island. But to write something out of one's own mind, worth reading for its own sake, is an arduous contrivance only to be achieved in fortunate moments, few and far

between. Personally, I would sooner have written "Alice in Wonderland" than the whole Encyclopaedia Britannica.[33]

Tangential to what Leacock says, Robertson Davies's essay, "Career of a Popular Humorist," concludes:

There are critics who sit in judgment upon a writer's life, sagely putting a finger on the point where he went wrong, was false to himself, let popularity and the flattery of publishers and public lead him from the strait path. Let such critics look to their own careers, if they have indeed careers to look to. It would certainly be better if a writer like Leacock knew always what was best to do and what would look best in the eyes of posterity, but such unnatural foresight cannot be required of any man.[34]

Perhaps Leacock's most enduring memorial, after his many books, is the annual Leacock Medal for Humour, established in 1946 by the Leacock Associates of Orillia. Humorists and professors of economics alike may take satisfaction in the knowledge that currently the Leacock Award carries with it a cash grant of $2,500.

CHAPTER 4

Grove to MacLennan

I think that at one time it was extremely difficult to be a Canadian writer. We still had for many, many years a kind of colonial mentality, a great many people felt that a book written by a Canadian couldn't possibly be good. It had to come from either New York or the other side of the Atlantic to be any good. This whole cultural climate has changed incredibly, and particularly in the last decade. My first book was published in 1960, and the change in those twelve years in the whole cultural situation in Canada has been enormous.

—Margaret Laurence (interview)

FOR the Canadian Midwest, and for the national literature in general, the decade 1915–1925 was an important one. As World War I increased in tempo, involving (after 1917) the United States as well as Canada, and during the years immediately following the Armistice in November 1918, writers treating a new region began to appear in rapid sequence. For example, Arthur Stringer's prairie trilogy (*The Prairie Wife*, 1915; *The Prairie Mother*, 1920; and *The Prairie Child*, 1922) shared attention with other Western novelists like Robert Stead (*The Homesteaders*, 1916; *The Cow Puncher*, 1918), the English visitor Harold Bindloss (*The Girl from Keller's*, 1917), Nellie McClung (whose first works predated the war years), new women writers such as Laura Salverson (*The Viking Heart*, 1923), and Martha Ostenso (*Wild Geese*, 1925, in which the harsh northwestern farming area brutalizes its inhabitants, destroying normal family ties), Hiram Alfred Cody (a clergyman originally in the Yukon whose long series of adventure-romances began with *The Frontiersman* in 1910), and others. For a time, it looked as if the focus of new fiction might be shifting westward together with the ever-moving center of population, but with the emergence of such figures as

Morley Callaghan, Mazo de la Roche, Hugh Garner, and Hugh MacLennan the urban East came in for more than enough attention to maintain a balance.

I *Frederick Philip Grove*

After the publication of *Over Prairie Trails* in 1922, Frederick Philip Grove—riding perhaps as much on a wave of awakening of public interest in his region as in the various conveyances that took him to his teaching assignments through frequent blizzards and routine snowdrifts—rapidly became one of the best-known writers in all Canada. Grove published between 1922 and 1933 a series of prairie novels that dominated the Midwestern scene as they aroused in himself a certain hubris that a less excitable and at times neurotic person might have escaped. He was given to dramatizing himself, partly through mystifications about his European origins, and apparently had considerable success in persuading others of his importance. *A Handbook of Canadian Literature* published in 1930 (by a firm in which, coincidentally, Grove had an interest) has high praise for all his fiction. In *Settlers of the Marsh* (1925), for example, he "revealed himself probably the supreme interpreter in fiction of Canadian prairie life, and no other aspect of Canadian life has been better done, if it has been done as well," etc. Then, in a revealing burst of critical enthusiasm the *Handbook* declares that "the fiction of Grove is the most serious rival of *The Golden Dog* for the supreme place in Canadian fiction."[1] (Earlier the same source had declared that Gilbert Parker's *Seats of the Mighty* was "not a serious rival to *The Golden Dog* for the honour of being the greatest Canadian novel.") A judgment that could dismiss with a wave of the hand all the fiction of Sara Jeannette Duncan, not to speak of several others, coupled with the opinion that William Kirby's *Golden Dog* was still "supreme," speaks eloquently for the state of Canadian literary history in 1930. On the other hand, what may be presumed to be Grove's last book—*Tales from the Margin*, a gathering of uncollected stories—was published as late as 1971. This event is in some measure, at least, an indication of his continuing reputation, after a whole new generation of prairie writers.

Grove did see the Midwest with intensity—appropriately enough, for it is a great cauldron of suddenly shifting intensities

within itself, politically, economically, emotionally. Even visually
he may have had some advantage in not having been British,
eastern Canadian, or Southern European in origin. (Recent
investigations by D. O. Spettigue have established that Grove was
not, as he claimed, the son of a bankrupt Swedish nobleman but
Felix Paul Greve, whose father was a minor official in Hamburg,
Germany.) "Direct aesthetic responses to the plains," Dick Harrison points out in *Unnamed Country* (1977), "in painting and in
fiction, reveal the same basic features as we have been looking at
in early first encounters with the prairie and in general cultural
responses to it—an initial difficulty in seeing the plains and a
tendency to impose familiar patterns on them."[2] Grove could
never be accused of seeing prairie life too rosily, as many early
settlers—homesteaders, investors in railroad lands, and other
optimists—often did. Like the American Frank Norris before him,
he was caught up in a kind of awe at the efforts on the grand scale
that produced torrents of wheat, and he could see the human toll
such efforts took. *In Search of Myself* and *Over Prairie Trails* both
reveal an inborn disposition toward the sombre view of human
affairs. This, applied to interpreting the inevitably harsh conditions of pioneer life, slanted Grove's work strongly in the direction
of naturalism, then a new note in Canadian writing but soon to
appear also in urban fiction. Discussing the place of settlement
hardships and settlement types in her well-known thesis-book
Survival (1972), Margaret Atwood points out that "most of our
good early-settler fiction deals with the prairies" where a good
many "will-driven patriarchs" appear and "one of the best places
to look for them is in the novels of Frederick Philip Grove."

There's Ellen's father in *Settlers of the Marsh*, clearing the land and
building his farm, praying fervently at night and proclaiming that God
has been good to him while at the same time driving his wife into the
ground by a combination of hard work, forced impregnation and equally
forced miscarriages. The father is imposing his pattern of straight lines—
barn, house, fence—in the curved land, and the wife and her fertility are
a part of the "curved" Nature he is trying to control. But instead of
controlling her he kills her, both spiritually (she comes to hate him) and
physically. He kills also the ability to love in his daughter Ellen. The
blockage of life-energy that results when Ellen refuses to marry the
protagonist finally precipitates a murder. There are the Clarks in *The
Master of the Mill*, in which the straight-line edifice is the mill and the
curve upon which it's imposed is the rest of life. There's John Elliott in
Our Daily Bread and Abe Spaulding in *The Fruits of the Earth*. In all

these cases the settlers succeed in their plan, build their straight-line constructions, but kill something vital in the process; it is often Nature in the form of a woman.[3]

Still Grove would hardly be read today if his work consisted in only such portraits. He had also the ability to describe the environment against which his characters pitted themselves, to make it almost at times a character in itself. He read and understood scientific theory enough for it to influence his outlook; and his philosophical determinism, for which he has been compared with Dreiser and Conrad, was strong, especially in his later works. The one novel displaying this side of Grove at length is *Consider Her Ways* (1947), which puts ants instead of anthropoids at the top of the biological stalk and uses their behavior to comment on that of humans.

One of Grove's latest biographer-critics, Margaret Stobie, sees in him a "reluctance to admit his limitations" along with "pretensions to experience or knowledge that he quite clearly did not have." She finds also, as other Canadian critics might, a dualism in his work,

a curious correspondence between the vision and its tawdry clothing in his writing . . . reflected everywhere in his work, in the two-part structure of most of the novels, in opposing modes of life, in fixed contrasts of characters, in the whole night-and-day, good-and-evil, Mary-Eve, either-or world that he creates.[4]

Prominent among other prairie writers of approximately the same time were Arthur Stringer, Robert Stead (discussed in Chapter 5) and Frederic Niven. Niven's *The Flying Years* (1935) presents a chronicle of how mid-nineteenth-century Canada became both a refuge and a land of opportunity for an evicted Scotch family, the Munros, in the Red River Settlement. It is the story of their son, Angus, whose own "flying years" span the era of change during which the buffalo vanish, the railroad arrives, the white man's disease debilitates the Indian. There are atrocities by both races but Angus, having had Indian wives, is disposed to take the Indians' side against the advancing hordes of white settlers, hungry for land. For instance:

Angus divided these immigrants in his mind (with his Indian kink) into two classes. Sooner or later in the chats there would be inquiry as to what he was about, driving through the land.

"Indian agent? Well, I got no use for the varmints. I left six *good Indians* down on my place in Nebrasky. Yes, sir, *good Indians*—down in the bottom of an old well there."

"Indian agent? There's a reservation near here, then, is there? Well, sir, that's good news. I don't know why it is but I like them folks. Danged if I don't even like the smell of them—wood-smoke, and the way they tan their deer-skins, and maybe a whiff of sweet-grass in their tepees, or some of the squaws with kinds of sachets of herbs stuck inside their clothes. Yes, sir, I'm darned if I don't like to see an Indian or two around."[5]

II   *Mazo de la Roche*

The same year that Grove published *Over Prairie Trails*, an eastern Canadian woman whose name was to become a household word brought out a book for juveniles called *Explorers of the Dawn*, about three motherless small boys in England with a governess, Mrs. Handsomebody, not governing very effectively. This received critical praise for its humor, especially as reflected in its skillful juvenile dialogue. This writer, however, was not destined to become another Lucy Maud Montgomery, although her success rivalled and at last surpassed that of the "Anne" books. She turned to the adult world and in a similarly related but much more protracted series built up a whole small world around Jalna and its variegated inhabitants among the Whiteoak family. After *Jalna* itself won the *Atlantic Monthly*'s $10,000 prize in 1927, the Jalna saga continued through a series of sixteen novels. The audience was international, largely but not exclusively women, and voracious for more and more chronicles: fan letters poured in by thousands, both appreciating performances already finished or asking for more and not infrequently suggesting directions in which the reader would like developments to flow. Not since Ralph Connor had there been quite such a phenomenon. "All in all," says Desmond Pacey, "it was a remarkably productive career, and marked the apogee in the history of the regional idyll in Canadian fiction."[6]

The carefully evoked setting of the series accounts for no small part of its success. To the various "Jalna" people, the established family and the old family mansion serve as social stabilizers—rather a different fictional use of the family home from that in the stories farther west, where, as Dick Harrison says, "the house becomes one of the most prominent symbols" representing prospective hopes of continuity and success but often serves in reality another purpose: "The number of unfinished, ruinous, or incongruous houses in the fiction implies a very elementary failure of the imagination," with the prairie the final victor.[7]

Other de la Roche books appeared as well, not all of them fiction, appropriately capped by an autobiography, *Ringing the Changes*, in 1957. George Hendrick sums up her contribution in these words:

Miss de la Roche's romantic imagination was perfectly attuned to the need of housewives, in whatever part of the world, to find imaginative surrogates for their humdrum lives. Judged not as a realist, not as a social critic, but as a writer of escape fiction, Miss de la Roche was a tremendous success. Her family dramas with their many erotic scenes provided wives and mothers with escape and entertainment. Read and admired by millions, she was for thirty years Canada's best-known writer. She had an eye for the comic, a fertile imagination, and the natural ability to tell a story. She did not seem to regard herself as a major writer; had she been under such a delusion, her life and work would appear tragic. As it was, after the success of the Jalna stories, she had several years of happiness with Miss Clement, their dogs, her adopted children. She had devoted readers who wanted to read more Whiteoak novels and not her other fiction. Her readers showed their admiration and devotion in their letters to her. Her publishers—Knopf, Macmillan, Little, Brown, and Company—had great prestige. She may not have written works as critically acclaimed as the Brontës, Dickens, and Galsworthy, but she clearly gave much pleasure to millions of readers. Such an achievement is, in itself, significant.[8]

Canada, along with its neighbors and more distant relatives, continues to produce novelists whose books find their way onto best-seller lists. One encounters among Canadian critics occasional words of praise for the craftsmanship of popular writers such as Thomas B. Costain or Arthur Hailey, but not much substantive comment on their works.

III *Morley Callaghan*

The first three novels of Morley Callaghan—*Strange Fugitive* (1928), *It's Never Over* (1930), and *A Broken Journey* (1932)— might be described either as apprentice-work or as a search for direction; probably they are both. The first two deal with criminality and violence in the bootleg era and owe something to Hemingway (whom Callaghan knew in Toronto) in subject and style. Social realism was a dominant mode at the time, as shown by John Dos Passos and James Farrell on the American side, or the work of Jessie G. Sime in Montreal: *Our Little Life* (1921). This novel, later acknowledged as the pioneer work in Canadian urban realism, uses as its plot-thread a quiet love affair between a middle-aged seamstress, Katie McGee, and a writer, Robert Fulton, an English immigrant, who completes a work on immigrants' experiences in Canada just before his death in the influenza epidemic of 1918. The alternative followed by some other novelists was satire, for which again an American parallel was present in Sinclair Lewis, and to a degree in Dos Passos. Toronto was the target of satiric novels by J. E. Middleton, Leslie Bishop, Francis Pollock, and Fred Jacob, whose *Peevee* was published the same year as Callaghan's first book. Peevee (for Pierre Vincent, surname Macready—all semi-symbolic names) begins as a writer but deserts literature for politics and journalism, picking up associates whose behavior offers ample scope for satire. Politics in Ottawa were similarly on view in Madge Macbeth's *The Land of Afternoon* (1924) and *The Kinder Bees* (1936). Callaghan, however, was not by inclination either a satirist or a sustained social critic; his natural sympathy for people, together with the Christian humanistic views that crystallized in him after an extended acquaintance with the philosopher Jacques Maritain, led him in other paths.

Early recognition of his abilities was not lacking. "No one today," declared Sinclair Lewis in 1929, "—if one may venture to claim Toronto as part of the American scene—is more brilliantly finding the remarkable in the ordinary than Morley Callaghan. Here is magnificently the seeing eye."[9]

With *Such Is My Beloved* (1934), Callaghan's main direction became established. A hero-priest, Father Dowling (at a discreet distance a Christ-figure), fails in his effort to rescue two prostitutes but after personal harassments including a term in a mental hospital, he receives mystical assurance of divine approval. Victory in defeat, saintliness in sinfulness, saving one's life by losing it—these were to remain the dominant themes of the later novels. In *More Joy in Heaven* (1937) the central problem is the ex-convict in society, represented by Kip Caley, who in his efforts to rehabilitate himself and at the same time help others, loses his life in circumstances that unjustly condemn him. *The Loved and the Lost* (1951) poses a choice to be made by the narrator, James McAlpine, between the security of social class, money, and political prestige and the apparently anarchic tastes of a girl he comes to love, Peggy Sanderson, a minister's daughter. Peggy accepts, for instance, the black society of Montreal. Confused and irresolute, McAlpine leaves Peggy to herself at what proves to have been a crucial time, for she is raped and murdered. The end finds McAlpine climbing, on a wintry morning, a street up Mount Royal, grieving and saying to himself:

When I knew I had her and could keep her, maybe I remembered that I too had come to Montreal to ride a white horse. Maybe that was why I was always trying to change her. That was the sin. I couldn't accept her as she was.[10]

The white horse is a symbolic reference, increasingly evident in Callaghan's novels: *The Many Colored Coat* (1960) uses the biblical Joseph story, and *A Passion in Rome* (1961) has the whole range of Roman Catholic symbolism and pageantry at its disposal. Of characterization in Callaghan, Edmund Wilson says:

His people, though the dramas they enact have more than individual significance, are never allowed to appear as anything other than individuals. They never become types or abstractions, nor do they ever loom larger than life. They are never removed from our common humanity, and there is never any simple opposition of beautiful and horrible, of lofty and base. The tragedies . . . are the results of the interactions of the weaknesses and strengths of several characters, none of whom is either entirely responsible or entirely without responsibility for the outcome that concerns them all.[11]

The theme of rejection versus acceptance which is so clearly evident in Callaghan's fiction takes on very broad proportions in the minds of Canadian critics, including Northrop Frye, whose approach is Jungian and thereby necessarily much involved with father-figures and others to be accepted or rejected. "The protagonist in Canadian literature," says D. G. Jones, "is asked to accept the North American wilderness in much the same way as Conrad's Marlow *[Heart of Darkness]* is asked to accept the African jungle. The little prairie town and Conrad's Brussels, Paris, or London are equally the embodiments of a garrison culture which will remain superficial and precarious until it has recognized and accepted the wilderness, not as something alien and exterior, but as an essential element in its own life."[12] Closer to home, Thoreau said the same thing earlier (in "Walking," for instance). In these symbolic terms the streets and ghettos of North American cities are cognate with wilderness, and the drama of acceptance/rejection may be played out there as truly as in the earlier poetry and fiction, either side of the international border, however much one might be tempted to prefer the howling wilderness of the forest to the roaring one of the city. This may be made to apply to Callaghan's latest novel, *A Fine and Private Place* (1975), which is set in Toronto during the late 1960s–early 1970s. The story begins with a developing romance between Al Delaney, a graduate student in English, and Lisa Tolen, researcher at a television station. Together they embark on a book about an eminent local novelist, Eugene Shore, finding the work so absorbing that they are in danger of losing one another until Shore's death in a hit-and-run accident. Al's final judgment on the man and his work is that

> . . . pushed to its logical conclusion Shore's world is a world of complete anarchy. Literature—anarchism's last hurrah! We knew about that. Yet it isn't true of Shore. There's the whole damned mystery. For some mysterious reason, it's something more than anarchy. I think I know why. I think it's some kind of warmth or love he has for all his characters, big or small, a love and respect for the mystery of the dignity of their personalities. . . .[13]

This applies very accurately to Morley Callaghan. Does it mean, as well, that we cannot draw completely logical conclusions about the world of art, or about life either? At least the "garrison culture" does so only at its own peril.

Summing up, we may look at two quotations from Callaghan, the first from one of his characters, the second direct from the man himself. Shore, the novelist portrayed in *A Fine and Private Place*, says:

> "I do my parables; I see little things happening." Shore went on. "I try and get them down. Maybe then some nut comes along and talks about symbols. Symbols? The whole thing is the symbol. The whole thing. If there's any magic it's in the way the imagination holds a life together. Yours as well as mine, Al. Maybe I see something in a bar or a cathedral. Maybe a man tells me a little story. . . something happening that bothers him. Now take my book. . . ."[14]

Finally, in 1971, the veteran of nearly fifty years' publishing speculates—more for his country than for himself—on what excellence means:

> The great thing about excellence is that it's never immediately recognizable. It's unfamiliar, naturally.
> But you must not misunderstand me, this is not a harsh view of Toronto or even Canada. Every country is in danger of going through this kind of thing. The thing is that you must not have the kind of nationalism which is an insistence on the protection of the third-rate, do you see? All you should say is, I know it's excellent, and the world will discover it *is* excellent. They'll discover it's Canadian, because they'll ask where it came from.[15]

IV   *Hugh MacLennan*

Keeping in mind the theme of acceptance/rejection which was seen to be so prominent in Callaghan, we encounter much of the same polarization in the fiction of Hugh MacLennan. Some of his upper-class characters well might, in fact, represent a "garrison culture" more obviously than Callaghan's; but in eastern Canada, and in Montreal especially (MacLennan's home and major focus), no ghost come from the grave, or critic either, is needed to tell us about tensions and conflicts. Anxiety, separation, aloneness— several of the titles of MacLennan's novels in themselves indicate how firmly these problems are mortised into his view of Canadian society: *Two Solitudes* (1945), *The Precipice* (1948), *Each Man's Son* (1951), *The Watch that Ends the Night* (1959, 1967). MacLennan has won the Governor-General's Award for fiction three times (1945, 1958, 1959), and is widely recognized as the ranking novelist of mid-century and afterwards. He writes, says Alec Lucas, to examine the philosophical-religious dilemma that the individual and the nation must wrestle with in determining a way or ways to live. Among the various causes of dislocation he "sees the need of man to take stock," and "his novels, as parables centred on religious humanism, go far toward performing this essential task."[16]

Out of what, then, does MacLennan construct his parables? Not very much out of academic life (although he is an academic himself), but rather political conflict and domestic emotional tensions of real magnitude. He uses physical violence and occasionally violent language, though on the whole he gives the impression of aiming for balance and restraint. Having tried the international novel in more than one early attempt (never published), he turned to Canadian society and in *Barometer Rising* (1941) used one of the most spectacular disasters in modern history as central event: the Halifax harbor explosion of December 5, 1917. This solves a number of the novel's plot complexities, most notably removing the stigma of military disobedience from Neil Macrae, whose accuser is killed in the blast. Critics have seen the book as an allegory of the collision between independence and conservatism, and certainly these traits are present in some of the characters, male and female alike. But whatever the allegorical ramifications may be, MacLennan's multifaceted descriptions of the events themselves are superb. For example:

> The pressure of the exploding chemicals smashed against the town with the rigidity and force of driving steel. Solid and unbreathable, the forced wall of air struck against Fort Needham and Richmond Bluff and shaved them clean, smashed with one gigantic blow the North End of Halifax and destroyed it, telescoping houses or lifting them from their foundations, snapping trees and lampposts, and twisting iron rails into writhing, metal snakes; breaking buildings and sweeping fragments of their wreckage for hundreds of yards in its course. It advanced two miles southward, shattering every flimsy house in its path, and within thirty seconds encountered the long, shield-like slope of the Citadel which rose before it.
>
> Then, for the first time since it was fortified, the Citadel was able to defend at least a part of the town. . . .[17]

Of the descriptive ability, so abundantly shown in *Barometer Rising*, the American critic Edmund Wilson says: "The imagination here for locality, for urban construction, for shipping surely reaches the point of genius . . . . the book is the work of a powerful poet who has mastered the materials of the engineer."[18] (Wilson feels that *Each Man's Son* and *The Watch That Ends the Night* are not so successful as *Barometer Rising*, and he is interested in *The Precipice* chiefly for its treatment of American culture.)

Two Solitudes, published four years later, presents not only the long-smoldering conflict between French and English segments in Quebec but rifts within the French community itself. Athanase Tallard, a man of influence who supports cooperation with English businessmen to develop Quebec, is condemned and ostracized; then when his influence declines he is deserted by the English as well. Parallel to his story is that of his son, Paul Tallard, who represents a racial union, or at least a compromise, half

French, half Irish. In *The Precipice* (1948) the protagonist, fed up with the narrowness of village inhibitions, leaves Canada for the United States only to reject American materialism at last for the simplicity of the Canadian woods. *Each Man's Son* (1951) is a less interiorized opposition which, in a Cape Breton mining town, sets the rationalist Dr. Daniel Ainslie against Archie MacNeil, a prizefighter whose violence leads to his own death together with that of his wife and another person. Dr. Ainslie adopts Archie's son Alan, who figures in *Return of the Sphinx* (1967); Alan, now grown and a successful politician—a cabinet minister attempting to bridge the French-English chasm—has a son Daniel who becomes a violent separatist and whose arrest forces his father's resignation along with a general family collapse. With "a strange little smile," Alan says to himself at the end, "One more step would have freed us all, but the sphinx returned."[19] This is an overt reference to the Oedipus legend, which MacLennan has consistently admired as "applicable to all times and places."[20] On the father-son relationship, Lucas remarks:

Most of MacLennan's characters have fathers who are stiff, if not tyrannical, frequently because they are puritans and generally because MacLennan depicts them as they appear to their sons. Thus, as normal in the young-man novel, they objectify the conflict within the psychology of maturing, the break that must occur so that the son himself may become an adult.[21]

One of MacLennan's strongest novels, *The Watch That Ends the Night* (1959), sets up a domestic problem in Montreal at the time of the Depression, Spanish Civil War, and advent of Hitler. George Stewart, a radio news analyst, has married the presumed widow of a friend, Dr. Jerome Martell, reported dead in Europe. But Jerome returns, adding to the already agonizing situation in which Catherine Martell-Stewart suffers from a chronic heart ailment. Thus, to a degree, MacLennan returned to the "international" novel which he gave up at the beginning of his career, although circumstances abroad are used chiefly as reasons for Jerome's departure and unexpected return, as if from the grave. The account of Jerome's early life in a New Brunswick logging camp is especially graphic, but that background is hardly the healing solitude of *The Precipice*. Nature is restorative for some persons, perhaps, but may be equally destructive or menacing for others. In this novel, as in some of the others, the journey motif is well employed, likewise the identity quest.

A moral issue—restoration of a man's reputation—is central to *Barometer Rising*. The fact that MacLennan is fundamentally concerned with the morality of his characters, or morality through them, is evident in such a meditative passage as this one from *The Watch That Ends the Night*. The thoughts are those of George Stewart, who has just witnessed what he takes to be the breakup of a marriage.

But that night as I drove back to Montreal I at least discovered this: that there is no simple explanation for anything important any of us do, and that the human tragedy, or the human irony, consists in the necessity of living with the consequences of actions performed under the pressure of compulsions so obscure we do not and cannot understand them. Morality? Duty? It was easy to talk of these things once, but surely it is no accident that in our time the best of men hesitate inwardly before they utter these words?[22]

Summing up MacLennan's achievements, George Woodcock felt (in 1969) that the bulk of his memorable work was contained in "three good novels" (*Barometer Rising, Each Man's Son, The Watch That Ends the Night*) together with the first half of a fourth, *Two Solitudes*. Despite limitations, "I cannot foresee a time when he will not be regarded as Canada's best social novelist, and—for all his manifest imperfections—as one of Canada's most considerable novelists of any kind."[23]

Interested primarily in urban people and their surroundings, MacLennan, like Callaghan, does not commonly use rural settings except those having to do with industrial operations or commercial developments. At the same time, nearly anyone living in Montreal can hardly escape the proximity of a still partly primitive nature, and we see this especially in the earlier part of *Each Man's Son* and the latter part of *The Precipice*. The continuing transition from rural to urban culture is a part of *Two Solitudes*. This theme, suggested in the present chapter by the grouping together of such writers as Grove, Callaghan, and MacLennan, will be the main concern of the next.

CHAPTER 5

Country, Town, and City

The land became more rolling, hummocky, confused, with bare cultivated spots, thick brush along random, half-concealed fences. The road and the river seemed to rival each other in the vagrancy of their courses. The banks were now white clay, now green with weedy grass or up-grown shrubbery, a brief row of tall trees—over all of which the sun flowed coldly. A man was tiny enough in the midst of great cities, he remembered strangely but here it was possible to wonder how many more of these roads there were stretching away into the evening, endlessly, bearing each its strung-out farms, its weight of enigmatic human and animal circumstance.

—Raymond Knister

UP TO this point in treating the development of Canadian fiction we have followed a linear pattern of description and analysis. This has extended over two centuries, bringing us now to a number of writers still living and writing. In the following three chapters, we encounter an efflorescence so extensive, as well as so near our own day, that it seems useful to enquire separately into some of the directions contemporary Canadian fiction has been taking.

The first in this trio of concluding chapters has a three-part pattern in itself. Social persistence and change reveal themselves through an inconclusive, uneasy dialogue among rural, urban, and superurban ways of living. The writers and their fiction thus examined are by no means unique to the problems they explore; they illustrate, of course, some of the "diversities" and often are themselves among the "searchers" appearing in the final two chapters. Despite this sorting-out for the sake of convenience, then, the reader will understand that virtually all the players are still on the field and the spectacle is really a continuing single game, not a tournament.

I *Country, in Several Keys*

In the works of Grove, as we have seen, the ominous or overpoweringly destructive character of Canadian prairie life received heavy emphasis. After Grove, writing about Canadian farm life could hardly avoid the stern challenge he gave it. Later developments have been approached by several writers, including two novelists, Edward McCourt and Henry Kreisel, who have produced important critical works. Kreisel sees puritanism (which the wide-ranging reader will readily perceive is by no means absent from the pioneering experience of the United States, South Africa, Australia, and New Zealand, among other "new" societies) as "one result of the conquest of the land, part of the price exacted for the conquest."[1] While conceding social and industrial changes, he finds it surprising that such novels as Adele Wiseman's *The Sacrifice* and John Marlyn's *Under the Ribs of Death*, published in the 1950s, and Margaret Laurence's *The Stone Angel* and *A Jest of God* along with George Ryga's *Ballad of a Stone Picker*, published in the 1960s, should have remained so close to the general pattern of earlier fiction. The explanation must be that change is slow: "Prairie puritanism is now somewhat beleaguered and shows signs of crumbling, but it remains a potent force still, and the vast land itself has not yet been finally subdued and altered."[2] Dick Harrison sees in many of the prairie works the same "imprisoned spirit" but at the same time examines both the romance and the sentimental comedy as counterweights. Novels in these latter modes, in addition to the earlier works of Nellie McClung and Ralph Connor, include *An Army without Banners* (1930) by John Beames, *The High Plains* (1938) by Wilfred Eggleston, *Especially Babe* (1942) by Ross Annett, *Peace River Country* (1958) by Ralph Allen, *Prairie Harvest* (1969) by Arthur Storey, and several by W.O. Mitchell, the best of the group.

Some years before Grove and others began their critique of prairie culture, Robert Stead's *The Homesteaders* (1916) had in effect homesteaded that fertile territory. Stead's forebears, as Susan Wood Glicksohn's introduction to a recent (1973) reprint of the novel points out, had had substantially the same experience as the fictional John Harrises:

Stead brings his family's story, and his own memories, to life. Pioneer conditions are vividly evoked, as are the physical details of life on even a prosperous ranch, the graceless routines which Beulah rejects as "making little twenty-four hour cycles that don't get us anywhere, except older."[3]

Frustration is very much in evidence in the fiction (both long and short) of Raymond Knister, a young writer whose premature death by drowning has been much lamented by his survivors and successors. A recent collection (1972) reprints six of the stories published during the early 1920s in various periodicals: "The One Thing," "Mist-Green Oats," "The Strawstack," "The Loading," "Elaine," and "The Fate of Mrs. Lucier." The first four deal with prairie loneliness and the "initiation" of adolescents, the final pair with women's mental disorders and with a brooding sense of evil. In one way or another all these stories express the dominant mood summed up by young Len at the conclusion of "Mist-Green Oats": "What's the use? What's the weary use?" Knister's novel *White Narcissus* (1929)—the title derives from the heroine's mother, who is obsessed with the flower—is a somewhat halting love story commingled with farm life. The beauty of the Ontario country-side, as seen during the lovers' long walks across fields and through woods, contrasts with the hard-slogging routine of daily work, described in this passage about oats-cutting:

> As before in the wheat-cutting, the three sizable Percherons could pull the binder only a few rods without weakening; and when the ponderous machine slowed, the broad drive wheel slid in the soft black soil, digging furrows a foot wide, almost that deep, and as many feet long as the horses could drag the binder thus, while the heads were torn from the stalks. Soon the field was spotted with these dark trenches, as though some preternaturally active rodent had been digging his home there in great numbers. And the horses were losing their freshness, even their willingness, as though they did not expect that their best efforts could cause the binder to run more than a few yards.[4]

This much, coupled with what has already been said about western-midwestern pioneering, is more than enough to validate Kreisel's thesis about prairie puritanism. How, then, were matters farther east? Two writers in the Maritimes, Will R. Bird and Thomas Raddall—both historically inclined—give us a less dismal picture even though the people they bring to life are from the age of puritanism in full cry. One of Bird's best-known novels, *Here Stays Good Yorkshire* (1945), appeared just at the end of World War II. Of the Yorkshiremen who emigrated to Canada during the years 1772-1776, Bird writes that they

. . .would not join the king's militia; nor would they support those who stood against the king. Necessity, that of planning crops that they might eat, of building roofs for shelter, of making furniture, beds, stools, tables and chairs that they might have more comfort, occupied their minds to the exclusion of all else, even to the greatness of their adventure. Nevertheless when Eddy's men began looting, irrespective of the householder's interest in the American cause, the Maccan Yorkshiremen presented such a united front that the raiders left them alone.[5]

They can be viewed in these terms partly because of their distance from us, no doubt; but here we have, as well, a strongly implied tradition not the same as that in the wheat and cattle country. The woman's side of life on the fur-trading frontier is explored by Pearl Packard in *The Reluctant Pioneer* (1968).

Thomas Raddall's *His Majesty's Yankee*, published in the grim war year 1942 (hardly the best time for a first novel to appear), treated events in Nova Scotia during the American Revolution with vividness and power, unmatched in his next two works *Roger Sudden* (1944) and *Pride's Fancy* (1946). Returning to this genre in 1960 with *The Governor's Lady* he regained some of his lost ground, as also in a book of stories, *At the Tide's Turn* (1959). And if a historical novelist can handle the past "with knowledge, understanding, humour, and affection," as Allan Bevan asserts Raddall can, he has too the advantage that

The stirring account of a pioneer society struggling for existence against savage men defending their rights and against an untamed wilderness of unfriendly rivers and of dark and foreboding forests, with the life-and-death-giving sea as their only connection with the civilization left behind, always appeals to some instinct in man.[6]

In *The Nymph and the Lamp* (1951) Raddall produced what is generally regarded as his best novel set in our own time. It is the familiar Canadian story of the wife caught in the loneliness of a place to which her husband's occupation takes her—to Susanna Moodie's backwoods, for example, or F. P. Grove's prairie—but this time it is a wireless station on Marina, an island off Nova Scotia. Seeming to lose her husband's love, Isabel Carney receives and accepts attention from Gregory Skane, one of the two other men on the island; then an accident sends her to the mainland for convalescence. As she is about to abandon all connection with Marina, news comes of a catastrophe—Matthew Carney's impending blindness—and she decides to return. Raddall's other novels with modern settings are *Tidefall* (1953) and *The Wings of Night* (1956). He has won the Governor General's Award three times and the Lorne Pierce Medal in 1956.

A much younger writer, George Ryga—best known as a dramatist, especially for television—has published *Ballad of a Stone Picker* (1966) and *The Hungry Hills* (1974). Both novels are set in the hardscrabble prairie country, the first being the story of two brothers, the elder of which (also the narrator) stays home:

> I'm alone with this farm, because I'm stupid and a little scared. I want to go some place—maybe just down the road no further than town. I want to stay . . . I don't know what I want to do.[7]

The younger brother, Jim, showed such great intellectual promise that he was given a Rhodes Scholarship, only to die by accident (or possibly by design—a suicide?) in England. Defeated and embittered, the remaining brother slogs on in a mood summed up beside his father's open grave, which he has dug himself:

> What price a stone-picker's ballad? What curse is his dream? What I saw and felt all these years was real—only to you, out there, was it wasted shadows on a landscape that has never been painted.[8]

The Hungry Hills returns its protagonist, Snit Mandolin, to rural Alberta after several years' absence. Work on a farm and in a town garage seems not to offer Snit what he wants, and he finally becomes involved with a bootlegger. In neither novel does the country appear to have very much to offer the descendants of the pioneers.

Two other novelists, by contrast, have been able to draw strength from association with the primitive. The first of these, Ernest Buckler, gives us part-realism, part-parable in *The Mountain and the Valley* (1952), a title which prefigures the division between apparent reality and the rare but all-embracing insight of mystical experience. David Canaan, the central figure, is a self-taught writer, having taken up the craft as an antidote to loneliness on his valley farm in eastern Canada. Ascending to a mountaintop on which he has a vision of the "single core of meaning," he longs to express this insight as a revelation to all, but, Moses-like, he does not reach such fruition; overstrained, his heart gives out and he dies—*on* the peak and *at* the peak.

Ox Bells and Fireflies (1968), although a personal memoir, contains numerous passages with a fictional cast insofar as technique is concerned. For instance:

> And once in your lifetime you had acted with real bravery.
> Walking ahead of the oxen down the mountain slope that day, with the neighbor (who'd swamped a road out while you chopped) riding on top the heavy pile of hemlock on the sleds, you heard him shout. The girdling chain had given way, pinning his foot between two shifting logs. If the whole load slid to the ground he would be crushed.
> You stopped the team and grasped the peavey, bracing it against the side of the load with more strength than you'd ever known you had. You held it there, though the load threatened to topple on you too. Straining until your muscles began to tremble. Praying that if you could "whoa" the oxen calmly enough they would not start ahead. The arteries in your neck began to pound, dizziness to swim in your eyes—but somehow you held the peavey there until your neighbor had unlaced his heavy army boot, drawn his foot out and jumped clear.
> It was less pride in yourself you felt than a kind of meekness. But when he put his arm around your shoulder and you saw that he was close to tears, that was a splendid moment too.[9]

The second of the pair, still another prairie writer, Robert Kroetsch, may be on the way to a possible synthesis of the various viewpoints about the land that we have found revealed. He is ready to use some of the newer, experimental techniques of fiction as well as an extended timespan. After his first novel, *But We Are Exiles* (1965—an adventure story using the exile motif, on several levels, about the crew of a boat making its way out of the Mackenzie River against both physical and emotional obstacles), Kroetsch began a prairie tetralogy. This, which includes *The Words of My Roaring* (1966), *The Studhorse Man* (1969), *Gone Indian* (1973), and *Badlands* (1975), has the ambitious intention of "laying out the timespan over which both historical and mythical shapes of the prairie past were formed."[10] The "roarer" of the first novel (the title is from Psalm 22) is a small-town undertaker named Johnnie J. Backstrom, who during the drought-ridden Depression years decides to enter politics, with unforeseen results including romance, violence, and great strain on a long friendship with (of all people) his political opponent. Johnnie tells his own story in language that sounds consistently like this detail from a political rally being addressed by a party leader:

Applecart was connecting Satan and all of hell with the dirty Eastern millionaires, the financial racketeers. He was the voice of the prairies speaking. He was ripping into all the betrayers of Christ and His holy principles which, it turned out, had a lot to do with the price of wheat and hogs.

My wife would not go away. She was supposed to be preparing coffee and cake for the guests. She had underestimated the crowd by thirty-five and was having loaves-and-fishes problems.

"How's the coffee coming?" I said.

"His Majesty wants more coffee," she said.

Sarcasm runs deep in the Burkhardts, especially in the women. I did not want more coffee. I was sick from too much coffee, among other things.[11]

Gone Indian, by contrast, is narrated by the letter method, in which an American professor (Binghamton State University, New York) writes to a girl in Notikeewin, Alberta, explaining the background of the death of a graduate student, Jeremy Sadness, who attempted to become an Indian. Jeremy's point of view is made available through excerpts from tape recordings made during his flight into the primitive.

Other recent prairie novels include Herbert Harker's *Goldenrod* (1972), using a horse-breaker as its central figure, and Ken Mitchell's *Wandering Rafferty* (1972), about an itinerant worker.

The Canadian primitive itself (what is left of it, which is still quite a lot) is the background to Fred Bodsworth's *The Strange One* (1959). In this Arctic idyll or "cold pastoral," a Scots biologist, Rory MacDonald of Barra (Hebrides) goes to the bleak James Bay muskeg country to band migratory geese. There he employs a young Cree Indian woman assistant, Kanina Beaverskin, with whom he falls in love and she with him. Their romance is paralleled by the story of a barnacle goose from Barra, lost in the vast Canadian wastes, where he mates at last with a Canada goose. Both plot-lines are reinforced by the beauty and strength of the surrounding natural world: nature here, it seems clear, is viewed as totally different from the implacable enemy conceived in so many Canadian works. It will be interesting to keep a story like this one in mind when we encounter Sheila Watson's *The Double Hook*, published the same year.

Closely related to the rural theme and sometimes included in it, but rising out of the industrial interpenetration of city and country, is the rising concern with environmental problems.

Usually this is expressed as part of some other topic, but occasionally may appear by itself, as in *The Lord's Pink Ocean* (1972) by David Walker, which envisions cataclysm through carelessness or indifference to chemical poisoning of the earth's total environment.

In the stories of Sinclair Ross, whose "town" novel will be looked at in the next section, town and country are interblended. The title story of *The Lamp at Noon* (1968) describes the mental breakdown of a farm wife during a dust-storm; in "A Field of Wheat," another woman suffers the same fate. "Cornet at Night," which foreshadows somewhat the novel *A Whir of Gold*, relates a young stranger's exceptional ability at music. In "Circus in Town" a small farm girl, deprived of a chance to see the real thing, creates a circus in her imagination. "The Painted Door," which is probably the best-known story of the collection, relates how a farm wife, suddenly unfaithful to her husband in the midst of a storm, is involuntarily implicated in his death. Assessing the total picture as given by Ross, Margaret Laurence says:

> The patterns are those of isolation and loneliness, and gradually, through these, the underlying spiritual goals of an entire society can be perceived. The man must prove absolutely strong, in his own eyes. The woman must silently endure all. If either cannot, then they have failed to themselves. With these impossible and cruel standards, and in circumstances of drought and depression, it is no wonder that individuals sometimes crack under the strain.[12]

II Town

Until after the depression years and World War II, towns and villages nearly everywhere still depended heavily on the surrounding countryside they were founded to serve. They took their beliefs and attitudes from the farm, and it was natural enough that their older populations should be made up chiefly of retired farmers and their longer-lived widows: cautious, frugal, sometimes pious, almost always set in their ways, characteristically suspicious of even minimal change. Here the tensions that so often marked rural life, most dramatically in the vast prairie and ranching heartland, were also present, and the novelists' responses were substantially those that characterized the "revolt from the village" in the fiction of Sinclair Lewis, Willa Cather, Sherwood Anderson, and other Americans from the 1920s onward. Among Canadian counterparts we shall look at three prominent representatives: Sinclair Ross, W.O. Mitchell, and Robertson Davies. The first two yield pictures of raw-boned prairie towns largely devoid of any pretense to art or other humanistic activity apart from straitlaced religion; the third, farther to the east, offers us in "Salterton" a larger, older Ontario town more on the order of Leacock's "Mariposa" which does aspire to culture but not with entire success. Although these three novelists are quite different in emphasis, all have been widely read and justly admired.

A   *Sinclair Ross*

Ross's *As For Me and My House* (1941) and the short stories contained in *The Lamp at Noon*, in the judgment of the historian of western Canadian fiction, Edward McCourt, "comprise the most significant body of prose fiction so far written about the prairie and its people,"[13] a judgment that Ross's recent works have rendered even more solid. In *As For Me and My House* the Reverend Philip Bentley is a deeply frustrated minister who wanted to be a painter, caught in a small Saskatchewan town during years of drought and depression. His agonies of spirit create tensions of spirit and aberrations in his wife as well, and their domestic life is incisively examined, as are their relations with the town and several friends within it. Failure and retreat seem to be inevitable consequences of such a situation. On the other hand, Ross is careful to point out, city life is by no means necessarily the saving alternative. Indeed, in *The Well* (1958) the central figure, Chris Rowe, is a fugitive from Montreal, healed by contact with the land, and in a *A Whir of Gold* (1970) a young musician from Saskatchewan, Sonny, is unable to come to terms with city life.

Ross's latest work, *Sawbones Memorial* (1974), invents a situation enabling him to characterize once more west Canadian small-town society (in "Upward," Saskatchewan, no more than a few hundred) at the same time offering a perspective of nearly half a century. After forty-five years' service as the town's only doctor, "Doc" Hunter is being given a farewell party at a new hospital named in his honor. As the entire town turns out to shake hands and chat with him over sandwiches and coffee, we survey— mosaic fashion, with the help of a few interior monologues—a half century of pioneering and immediately post-pioneering experience and are invited to judge whether or not Upward has gone very far in the direction its name implies. The answer is both yes and no; the author, like his protagonist, is skeptical of the town's official opinions of itself but not ready, either, to condemn it out of hand. In the process of building his mosaic, Ross has managed the considerable feat of competing with his earlier, much-heralded success on equal terms: *Sawbones Memorial* is a work to be read alongside *As for Me and My House* as no muted encore. Its method is different but its style remains sharp-set, its characters very much alive, its conclusions largely the same after testing by time. All this gives the book uncommon interest and testifies to the increasing durability of Canadian literary talent.

B   W.O. Mitchell

Just as Ross's *Sawbones Memorial* in its account of Doc Hunter's practice takes a less encapsulated view than *As For Me and My House*, W.O. Mitchell's chief novel, *Who Has Seen the Wind* (1947), is set in part-town, part-prairie, in the late 1920s and into the Depression. Taking young Brian O'Connal from early boyhood to maturity, the story is narrated in easy descriptive style with plenty of detail to reinforce the central thread of Brian's responses to people and surroundings as he grows up. "Characters" and eccentrics abound—a blasphemous Uncle Jean; a philosophical shoemaker; Saint Sammy ("Jehovah's Hired Man") who lives on the prairie in a piano-box; Miss Thompson, the courageous schoolteacher; Peter Svarich, the Ukrainian doctor; Old Ben and Young Ben—a full gallery. Strong single episodes likewise help to develop a balanced account of prairie life, finally rather more positive than negative as shown in Brian's final commitment to the prairie when he resolves to become an agricultural researcher, a "dirt-doctor." Mitchell's other fiction, not surprisingly, reveals a parallel commitment on the author's part. *The Kite* (1962) takes a city journalist to a small town to interview the oldest living Canadian; in the process, he learns a great deal about many more of the town's inhabitants. Mitchell's novel on Indian life, *The Vanishing Point* (1973), will be discussed in Chapter 6.

C   Robertson Davies

A very different town scene forms the background to the "Salterton" novels (loosely a trilogy) of Robertson Davies. "Salter-

ton," not unlike Leacock's "Mariposa," is a well-established Ontario town on its way toward being a small city in the next
generation—not a boondocks wheat depot as in Ross's fiction, but
no Athens, either, despite its pretensions. The first novel of the
series, *Tempest-Tost* (1951), might be described as *Teapot-
Tempest-Tost*, for its main action centers in a local production of
The Tempest in which all that may so easily go wrong in Little
Theater—with the productions themselves and the people who
stage them—does go wrong. Davies's rich and extensive experience
in the theater undoubtedly contributed heavily to the authenticity
of detail in this delightful comedy. *Leaven of Malice* (1954,
winner of the Leacock Award in that year) will be discussed under
the heading "Academic Life" in Chapter 7. *A Mixture of Frailties*
(1958) takes a young Salterton girl, Monica Gall, to London as a
music student. There, her associations give Davies a chance to
return to the artistic world of London which he knew as an actor
and director at the Old Vic before World War II, and he develops
both comedy and romance against this background.

III *City*

The very first Canadian novel came from a city, at least
technically speaking, and Frances Brooke's opinions of the local
peasantry reflected a kind of country-city opposition which of
course is ancient and universal. In the ensuing two centuries there
has been extensive urban growth in eastern Canada: Quebec,
Montreal, Toronto, Halifax, Ottawa, Hamilton—all these places
have grown tremendously. Not only do the great majority of
Canadians live within a few hundred miles of the United States
border, but adding farther western cities like London (Ontario),
Winnipeg, Calgary, and Vancouver, a very large part of the urban
majority will be found in these and other cities. Some of these
places have become literary centers, Halifax (with Joseph Howe,
Thomas Chandler Haliburton, and others) having been the earliest but now surpassed by Montreal and Toronto, both publishing
centers. Most Canadian cities have become, by now, settings for
stories and novels, the favorites being Montreal (with MacLennan, Metcalf, Richler, for example), Toronto (Garner, Callaghan),
and Vancouver (Lowry, Wilson).

Montreal began to find a place in realistic fiction with Jessie G.

Sime's *Our Little Life* (1921), which describes the grubby routine of lower middle class Montreal. Even here, however, there is the possibility of limited intellectual survival, as shown not through a romance but a companionate liaison between a seamstress, Katie McGee, and an immigrant writer, Robert Fulton, who reads Katie chapters of a book about immigration to Canada. Miss Sime herself was an immigrant from Scotland during World War I. A book of her stories, *Sister Woman*, appeared in 1920, developing against the same background a sustained plea for the 1920 version of women's liberation. Despite such a lead, however, the direction taken in these works was not to be followed, in Montreal, until the times of the next world war, when several more prolific writers began using that city as their locale. The fascination Montreal has had for writers is well illustrated in Hugh Hood's descriptive work, *Around the Mountain* (1967), subtitled "Scenes from Montreal Life."

Another woman writer, Irene Baird, published in 1939 a much-praised study of Vancouver in the 1930s, *Waste Heritage*. Gangs of unemployed young men assemble and disperse uneasily until, in the climactic episode, there is a violent confrontation in Hastings Street, Vancouver, in 1938. The mood of the period is apparent in these samples of the narrative:

"There was this big jobless demonstration going on in front of the city hall and someone threw a rock and they called the riot squad. I got smacked on the head by a riot stick. That was the first time I ever got blind-mad in my life. . . ."[14]

A man with a long thin nose and eyeglasses, who looked like a ratepayer, spoke up from the other end of the room. 'If you ask me,' he said, 'the most of these men don't want work. If they'd wanted work they'd have gone out and rustled for it, not waited around to be spoon-fed by the government.' He got up, came along, and flipped down his quarter [for a meal in Cal's Coffee Counter].
    Matt stood up as he passed, 'Did you ever try it?'
    'Try what?'
    'Lookin' for work.'
    Ruddy-face swung round on his stool. 'Are you one of the sit-downers?' he asked with interest.
    'Never mind that,' Matt said, 'I asked this man a question.'[15]

In a previous novel by Baird, *John* (1937), an English business-man, abandons his world for sanctuary in British Columbia.

Hugh Garner, who has lived in Toronto since the age of six, shares with Morley Callaghan an abiding interest in that city. His best-known work, *Cabbagetown* (1950; 1968 in longer form) is set in the Depression years, with three chronological divisions: Book I, Genesis, March 1929–June 1932; Book II, Transition, June 1932–October 1933; Book III, Exodus, October 1933–February 1937. Its events include petty crimes and not-so-petty, protest meetings, and the departure of young Canadians to serve in the international brigades of the Spanish Civil War. Typical characters are migrant workers and adolescent lovers. Two other books, *Present Reckoning* (1951) and *The Yellow Sweater and Other Stories* (1952), are closely related to *Cabbagetown* in the sympathy they express with working people, as are such later novels as *The Silence on the Shore* (1962), set in a Toronto rooming-house of the 1950s, with a set of native and immigrant characters, most of them lonely and suffering from various mental or physical ailments, and *The Sin Sniper* (1970), a crime story set in the "Moss Park" area of Toronto. Of "Cabbagetown," Garner wrote: "Toronto's Cabbagetown remains only a memory to those of us who lived in it when it was a slum. Less than half a mile long and even narrower from north to south, it was situated in the east-central part of the city. . . . Cabbagetown, before 1940, was the home of the social majority, white Protestant English and Scots. It was a sociological phenomenon, the largest Anglo-Saxon slum in North America."16 A collection, *Hugh Garner's Best Stories*, won the Governor General's Award for 1963. A later collection, *Violation of the Virgins* (1971), contains stories with settings as diverse as West Virginia, Miami, the American Southwest, eastern Canada, and a Caribbean ship. Five years after Garner's first publication of *Cabbagetown*, Earle Birney in *Down the Long Table* (1955) described the hopelessness of unemployment during the Depression and satirized some of the too-easy liberalism of the times, as viewed from western Canada.

Other writers using the Toronto setting include Llew Devine, with *The Arrow of Apollyon* (1971), describing the Toronto stock exchange and setting a murder story against its background, and Richard Wright, whose *The Weekend Man* (1970) looks in upon the tangled day-to-day life of Wes Wakenham, a publisher's salesman living in a Toronto suburb. The weekend man, says Wes,

. . . simply never learns to live with the thundering ironies . . . . What to do? Well, you'll have to work it out for yourself. I myself just drift along, hoping that the daily passage will deliver up a few painless diversions. Most of the time, however, I am quietly gritting my teeth and just holding on.[17]

Industrial life farther to the north and east enters into Percy Janes's *House of Hate* (1970), set in "Milltown," Newfoundland, a papermill industrial town. Rather than centering in labor troubles or the like, it is a family story, the chronicle of Saul and Gertrude Stone, Irish immigrants. Saul—Dad—is more cruel than kind; four of his five sons have been marked for life by "the strange fatal lethargy which the spewing forth of a father's indiscriminate hate had cast over the will of each of them."[18] The chief aim of the book is to explain the processes by which such violent hatred operates. The stories of J. Michael Yates's *The Man in the Glass House* (1968) are city-born parables of crowds, lost individuals (for example, in the airport, the "glass house"), photography, disc-jockeying, etc. Finally, this sampler series may be brought to an end with John Metcalf's *Going Down Slow* (1972), whose hero David Appleby, a high school teacher in Montreal, has emigrated from England only to find himself unable to come to terms with North American life, in contrast with his roommate Jim, who does. As a result, he "spends a disturbing amount of his time plotting the destruction of his enemies, and too little time securing his own viable future,"[19] one critic thinks.

By coincidence, at the back of a Mordecai Richler paperback the name Juvenal appears, the only ancient represented in a list of the publisher's authors. On the basis of works like *The Incomparable Atuk* (1963) or *Cocksure* (1968), linking Richler with Juvenal would be natural enough; but whereas the Roman is angered over a lapse of moral standards that presumably might be reestablished, his modern counterparts such as Huxley, Richler, or Kurt

Two writers of very considerable output are closely associated with Montreal: Mordecai Richler and Hugh Hood. Richler, the more cosmopolitan of the pair, lived in London for quite a few years but has recently returned to Canada, and has consistently used both Canadian characters and behavior in his extended satirical skirmishing with his native land. *The Apprenticeship of Duddy Kravitz* (1959), his most appealing work, will be discussed in the context of the Canadian-Jewish novel in Chapter 6; here, three other books dealing with city life (characteristically, not all about Montreal) are to be looked at.

Vonnegut would not be nearly so sure of that. *Cocksure* is Juvenalian enough in the way it portrays the swinging "in"-set of London, who are a mélange of the Continent, Hollywood, and whatever other status symbols are/were current—as for example in this snapshot of the Star Maker's entry into London as part of a caravan not many units short of a full-dress circus parade:

> Everybody at the morning conference got up to look. On the street below a motor cavalcade passed. Two men on motor-cycles were followed by a Silver Cloud Rolls Royce, an ambulance, a Brinks-type armoured car, two Austin Princesses, a refrigeration truck and two more men on motor-cycles.[20]

The Star Maker plays spider to the general web of perversion in which the characters find themselves; a fair sample would be Chapter 10, which describes a screening of a "new-wave" film entitled "Different," directed by one of the widest swingers of the set, Ziggy Spicehandler. The protagonist (if any character in such a phantasmagoria can be so called) is Mortimer Griffin, a Canadian who has a good position with a London publisher but still suffers various traumas over the state he must live in, that is, mandatory liberation into compulsory freedom. In all, *Cocksure* stands at the end of the sexy 60s as a satiric compendium of what many other authors were solemnly taking as—for all they could tell—the permanent new life-style.

But if London seems thus decadent (and it certainly does), what of the presumably less corruptible New World? To this, Richler had already supplied an answer in *The Incomparable Atuk*, in which an Eskimo poet is to nearly everyone's delight "discovered" and brought to Toronto, even as eighteenth-century "savages" (presumed noble savages) were brought to European capitals, mostly as curiosities. In Atuk, both the curious and the believers in primitive innocence get more than they bargained for. Instead of being repelled by commercialized Canada, he loves it, using and improving the opportunity of his sensational reception for all it is worth. He brings his whole family to Toronto, installing them in comfort and refusing to leave; thus the frenetic media, caught by their own publicity gimmicks, are nonplussed as to what to do until in a drastic way out they stage (on television) the ultimate of all gimmicks and rid themselves of this turbulent poet. Part III, "This Was the Noblest Canadian of Them All," is a completely

ironic subtitle so far as Atuk is concerned, but it is aimed even
more directly at his mush-minded exploiters and instant admirers.
St. Urbain's Horseman (1971)—St. Urbain is one of the principal streets of older Montreal—marks the end of Richler's exile as
well as a return, temporarily at least, to the emphasis on character
analysis of *The Apprenticeship of Duddy Kravitz*. Perhaps it
illustrates better than some of Richler's earlier novels his stated
belief that "any serious writer is a moralist, and only incidentally
an entertainer."[21] In speaking of the large element of fantasy in
Richler, George Woodcock remarks that it persists in this novel
"but its monsters do not walk like badly jointed carnival figures
through the physical scene."[22] This novel, Richler's longest and by
consensus his best work thus far, is the story of Jake Hersh, a TV-
film director in London, originally from St. Urbain's, Montreal.
Jake fantasizes a wild-man cousin, Joey, who hunts down in
Paraguay a Nazi war criminal and is an enviably fine horseman,
only to be killed, ironically, in an air crash. Jake somewhat
inexplicably continues a friendship with Harry Stein, whose
escapades involve them both in a sex-and-drug trial at the Old
Bailey. Duddy Kravitz is also, briefly, a character in the novel.
The end sees Jack still in a much-troubled mental state:

He wept because the Horseman, his conscience, his mentor, was no more
. . . . I will be St. Urbain's avenging Horseman. *If*, a more skeptical voice
intruded, *there ever was one* . . . . What if the Horseman was a distorting
mirror and we each took the self-justifying image we required of him?[23]

Hugh Hood's work uses both Montreal and Toronto as its
background. After a book of stories, *Flying a Red Kite* (1962), he
published two novels dealing with the arts, *White Figure, White
Ground* (1964, on painting) and *The Camera Always Lies* (1967,
on film-making). The plot ramifications of *A Game of Touch*
(1970), a story told in first person, enable Hood to do a good bit
with the Montreal setting, including its tortured politics. It
introduces young Jake Price, a country boy from Ontario and new
to Montreal, to an informal group playing touch football, one of
whom is a political figure named Roger Talbot. As an aspiring
cartoonist (one of whose satirical drawings got him expelled from
school), Jake finds his talent useful to Talbot and others. At length,
Talbot is forced out of the race for power, and at the end a whole
network of personal relationships seems to be disintegrating. The

problems of Quebec, Jake learned, often centered in great numbers of ordinary people

. . . who had patiently and silently endured degraded lives while their neighbours, sometimes their next-door neighbours, enjoyed things they could not have. A man could go back and forth from a small house, av|enue de la Roche, to a soft-drink bottler's in the Town of Mount-Royal, all his life, and be paid less for the same work than an *anglophone* across the room. A few years back some Québecois had been attaching a metal strip to their license plates with CENT ANS D'INJUSTICE written on it. *And they had meant it.* [24]

These are the people who figure most frequently in both Hood's stories and his novels, whether they are set in Montreal or Toronto. *You Can't Get There from Here* (1972) turns ostensibly to Africa, satirizing neocolonial jockeying for power in "Leofrica," a federation of two dramatically different states recalling perhaps the Canadian "problem" as well.

The Swing in the Garden (1975) is the first in a series of twelve novels Hood has set himself to publish during the remainder of the century. They will cover Canadian life, presumably, from the 1930s (the time of the first novel) through the 1990s. Taking Proust as his model, Hood presents, through his narrator Matthew Goderich (born in the early years of the Depression), a closely observed "documentary" story, packed with frequently minute detail and teeming with characters. Political questions enter here, as well—through Matthew's father, a philosophy professor who resigns his position as a matter of ethical principle when politics become intolerably crass to him—and through the son's own perplexities:

I wondered why there was this preoccupation with Scotchness, or Scotticism if you prefer, in the post-colony of my boyhood. Why were perfectly un-Scots boys like Bob Silcox strutting up and down on the greensward of the Lacrosse Grounds in kilts, to the truly dreadful sound of badly played bagpipes (think of Haydn's use of the drone bass in his *Bear* symphony and then think of the St. Andrew's College Pipe Band), with sporrans and some sort of ludicrous large safety-pin affixed to the material of the plaid? Why were the leading militia regiments of the city apt to be kilted, as were the Toronto Scottish, the Forty-Eighth Highlanders, even the Irish Regiment? Why, for that matter, was the annual display of military pomp in Toronto called the Garrison Parade? God knows, the garrison mentality has been often enough attributed to the small ruling class of Ontario society as it then was, beset by Indians, and worse, by French. The name of the parade betrayed the reality of the syndrome.[25]

Not surprisingly, this novel won the City of Toronto Literary Award in 1976. One hopes that if indeed the twelfth novel of the series appears in or near the year 2000, when Hood will be 72, a very special party will occur on the day of its publication (in whatever format the written word by then may take). Harry Bruce describes, admiringly, Hood's fiction as "introspective journalism," making little or no distinction between that term and "fiction." Asking whether or not novelists like Dickens, Proust, and Dreiser had not been journalists as well, he says he thinks that "the handy distinction between fiction and journalism is often very wrong and . . . in recent years, it has been wrong more often than ever before."[26]

Separatist violence in Montreal could hardly go unnoticed by novelists of the past few years. One response, *The Lonely Ones* (1969) by James Bacque, involves two friends, both artists and nature lovers, who together with a girl from England are swept into a bomb-plot to assassinate the Prime Minister. The action takes place primarily in Montreal and in the Laurentians to the north, where they retreat to a cabin by a stream. Finally, when as fugitives in a car they approach Toronto, that city appears to them in this light:

Feared Toronto on the horizon suddenly. My metropolitan hatred. On this slanting downward hillside towards the night-time west, towers bluntly rising from the far grass. The new light on them. Stop to stare over the sleeping hillside of houses and green lawns scarcely awakening into the built promise of the city. . . . City which I have never imagined, unimaginable Toronto, give us a home. Don't betray us. And along smooth highways with our shadow running widely ahead of us trying to catch the next breath of road jittering in the speed. Fender mirror bloated with the gold bright sun behind it. It will have to be Michael in this city where we are at last not known.[27]

Bacque holds little hope of any help from France for an independent Quebec; neither does Eric Koch in *The French Kiss* (1968), which satirizes De Gaulle and Gaullism. John Mills's *October Man* presents the Quebec "October crisis" of 1970 as seen from the Montreal underworld. Dollar signs on the title page help emphasize the theme.

CHAPTER 6

Leacock's Successors

Apart from Robertson Davies, the record of humorous writers is much less encouraging—so unpromising, indeed, that the prematurely established Stephen Leacock Medal for humor is at present [early 1960s] an annual embarrassment.

—Hugo McPherson

BETWEEN Haliburton and Leacock there was not very much Canadian humor of high quality: the American movement that Haliburton so accurately gauged and admired—the New England Yankee and Old Southwestern strains alike, culminating in Mark Twain—had no counterpart in the north. Leacock's work helped mightily to thaw what must have seemed a kind of permafrost, and since his day (he was active from 1910 until the 1940s) there have been humorists in plenitude, even though their efforts have received scant critical praise. Hugo McPherson, quoted above, did have some good words for W.O. Mitchell's *Jake and the Kid* (1961) and Paul Hiebert's *Sarah Binks* (1947), both winners of the Leacock Medal and presumably at least not so embarrassing as some others. But the fact that humor is notoriously evanescent and hard to judge is no prohibition against rewarding its hard-working practitioners; and one may observe that with the passing of time, some of the winners of the more prestigious Governor General's Award for fiction are no longer remembered with awe and amazement. Also, of course, humor has been an ingredient in the work of novelists whose intentions have not been primarily humorous or satirical—for instance, Sara Jeannette Duncan, Nellie L. McClung, or Will R. Bird. This brief survey-chapter will serve to show, by listing a number of writers and titles and discussing a few, what the range of subjects among Canadian humorists has been during the past forty to fifty years.

Leacock's *Sunshine Sketches* were not without occasional bite, and other small towns, especially such as pretended to culture that they did not really have, came within the gunsights of satirists: William Arthur Deacon's *The Four Jameses* (1927), Victor Lauriston's *Inglorious Milton* (1934), Paul Hiebert's *Sarah Binks* (1947), and Robertson Davies's *Tempest-Tost* (1951) together with companion volumes of his "Salterton" triptych. Other writers have taken a broader canvas in displaying social and political life in various segments of Canada: Madge Macbeth looks sharply at Ottawa in *The Land of Afternoon* (1924) and *The Kinder Bees* (1935); Fred Jacob (*Peevee*, 1928) and Leslie Bishop (*The Paper Kingdom*, 1936) at the Toronto literary world; J. E. Middleton (*Green Plush*, 1932, and *The Clever Ones*, 1936) at Toronto business life. Farther west, British Columbia received a share of attention in Magnus Pyke's *Go West, Young Man, Go West* (1930) and John Cornish's *The Provincials* (1951). Adding to the variety have been works on the Depression and World War II—Earle Birney's *Down the Long Table* (1955) and *Turvey* (1949); the newspaper world and the politics it mirrors—Bruce Hutchison's *The Hollow Men* (1944), Ralph Allen's *The Chartered Libertine* (1954), and William Weintraub's *Why Rock the Boat?* (1961); the film industry, most specifically Hollywood—Hugh Hood's *The Camera Always Lies* (1967), Mordecai Richler's *Cocksure* (1968), Timothy Findley's *The Butterfly Plague* (1969), and Rachel Wyatt's *The String Box* (1970). A spectrum of attitudes about some of these subjects along with others, ranging from affected scorn to joy in pure anarchy, appears in the novels of a number of younger writers to be mentioned in Chapter 8. Now for a closer focus upon a few of those listed above.

Even if the author of *Sarah Binks* (1947) had not stated so positively that his poetess-heroine, widely known as "The Sweet Songstress of Saskatchewan," was by her own testimony a "daughter of the Old South" (her parents came north from South Dakota), the reader of *Huckleberry Finn* would feel certain that she must have been a first cousin to the late Emmeline Grangerford, whose lyrics Huck so much admired and transcribed. As for that, "internal evidence," as the scholars say, is enough in itself. The final stanza of Sarah's *Song to the Four Seasons* reads:

> A long, quiet winter with plenty of snow,
> And plenty of barley; it's eighty below,
> Barley in the heater, salt pork in the pantry—
> How nice that you never feel cold in this country.

(A footnote explains: "It is in rhymes such as these, 'country' made to rhyme with 'pantry' that Sarah reveals herself as a daughter of the Old South.")[1] A trip to Regina (in 1926) and an affair there with "Henry Welkin, aesthete, patron of the arts and letters, and travelling salesman" brought Sarah into a literary decline (chapter 8, "The Dark Hour") from which she rallied to win the poetry competition at the Quagmire Agricultural Society Fair and was awarded as her prize a handsome horse thermometer. From this success she went on to win the Wheat Pool Medal for an epic entitled *Up from the Magma and Back Again*. Contemplating the possibility that her career might suffer from too much fame too soon won, she wrote, not long before her death:

> This makes me scratch myself, and ask,
> When shall my powers fade?
> It puts me severely to the task,
> To face this fact undismayed.[2]

And what of her death itself?

"This makes me scratch myself and ask"; the Fates weave their web or circumstance around the great. It is no mere coincidence that the great epidemic of hives which swept Saskatchewan should have found Sarah with a horse thermometer which registered six degrees too high. It is no mere coincidence that she had become passionately fond of Scotch mints, and bearing down upon one of them at a moment when she was taking her own temperature cracked the thermometer and swallowed the mercury, a full tablespoon with a plop. There was no catching it. Death loves a shining mark; the Fates had tied the final knot in the web—and in Sarah. For her there was no escape.[3]

Hiebert provided a sequel to *Sarah Binks* with *Willows Revisited* in 1967.

Two years later the winner of the Leacock Medal, Birney's *Turvey* (1949), subtitled "a military picaresque," remains close to the often absurd routine of military life as seen by the common soldier. Still, it is a toss-up as to whether Private Turvey—whose career before enlistment for World War II has already been enough of a civilian picaresque all over Canada to baffle the psychiatric officers—endures more because he is in the Canadian army, or the army because he is in it. One does not forget that this is a poet's story and that poetry and humor rise from the same spring; that if Aristophanes or Chaucer had been in the infantry during World War II, as Birney was, he would have looked hard, listened hard, and given us (profanity and all) something very much like *Turvey*, which predates its more famous (but not funnier) North American relative, *Catch-22*, by over a decade. The following passage will give some idea of Turvey in his usual role of more-sinned-against-than-sinning. When Potts, "a serious-minded Ordnance Clerk who had recently been assigned to type psychological reports for the Personnel Officer," tells Turvey during an evening mess in England, that he's "too full of aggression" Turvey counters that he only wants some excitement but the "Only difference bein a soldier over here is I have to roll down a flock of skewgee old blackout blinds at night and roll em up in the mornin." [Birney, a very careful student of speech-rhythms both as poet and linguist, uses near-phonetic notation which has no use for apostrophes.] He hasn't even been to London yet:

> ". . . I aint ever seen a nair-raid, or—or," Turvey groped for a worthy alternative, "or the Bloody Tower."
> "There you go," Potter hissed; he was a little man who packed a great deal of energy into his speech. "Always thinking *violently*. Blood and bombs and things. You should realize it's our *duty* as Canadian soldiers to—to *channel* our own aggressions, see, *channel* em. We gotta save up our frustrations—" he paused and thrust his little round chin across the table at Turvey—"to smash the Nazis with."
> Turvey felt vaguely he hadnt made himself clear. He swallowed the last forkful of spam and looked at his dessert. "Custard again," he sighed.
> Potts, who had forgotten to eat, regarded him with bright frantic eyes. "Custard, sure, custard! *That's* the real adventure right now. Stop being a *Canadian*. Powdered egg omelet and custard and spam and hardtack and—and—basic training over and over again, and putting up with our officers—"
> "What about sergeants?"
> "*And* sergeants. Dont you see? That's *our* part of the Battle of Britain! We learn how to suffer, to—to channel. We *discipline* our energies."
> Turvey abstractedly wiped his cheek from the spray of Potts' intense vocables. . . . [4]

Later warfare, even less reasonable than Turvey's version of World War II, is the background of Charles Dennis's *Stoned Cold Soldier* (1973) which tries hard but falls considerably short of being a new *Turvey* or *Catch-22*.

Just as personal discomfiture is the matrix of *Turvey*, so it is in Farley Mowat's *The Boat Who Wouldn't Float* (1970), still another Leacock medalist. In this chronicle of wasted time the author of a number of well-known nature works relates his difficulties with a secondhand boat (bought after drinking "screech" on the south shore of Newfoundland on a rainy night) refitted and christened *Happy Adventure*. On the way to Expo 67, for example (where the craft performed no better than at other places), this exchange takes place:

> Three hours later I was roused from my gloomy ruminations below decks by a hail from the wharf.
> "Is that the boat called the *Unhappy Misadventure*?"
> Now I occasionally allow myself to say uncomplimentary things about my vessel, but no one else is going to do it with impunity. Stung to the quick I leapt up the companionway.
> "Who the hell wants to know?" I yelled angrily.[5]

The Big Stuffed Hand of Friendship (1969) by Norman Newton takes place in the British Columbia coastal town of Pt. Charles, where on the timber wharves or in fish canneries Indians and Chinese find work, with resultant social tensions. School, church, sexual mores, and local politics all come up for their lumps, as well as the Canadian literary establishment as seen in a hilarious poetry conference (Chapter 11) of which this excerpt is a fair sample:

> Little Earl Pertwee, who hunched frog-like near one end of the table, his chin resting on his hands, his huge glasses seeming to cover most of his tiny flat face, hopped into the breach.
> "Poetry," he said, "is the prose of the inarticulate."
> It was the one remark he had come prepared with, and his chief worry was that, out of nervousness, he would commit a spoonerism, and spoil its effect. Having uttered it successfully, he settled back on himself with a self-approving glare.
> "Oh, *nonsense!*" cried Terence Wadsworth angrily. It was most unfair. He was the only epigrammatist in Canada.
> "Poetry is the genitals of the soul," said Milton Koshevoy. Milton was a little more up to date than Bernard, who was still wrestling with the corpse of a moral system which had been dead for some time.
> "I think we're beginning to drift away from the subject," said Dr. MacDonald, nervous that this remark might incite Bernard to a new attack on Puritanism, and a cascade of four-letter words.[6]

Newton's big stuffed club of satire has some sharp-cornered rocks distributed among its rags and cotton-batting.

Much of the humor in *Them Damned Canadians Hanged Louis Riel!* (1971) by James McNamee is implicit in the title. Told through the eyes of a young nephew of Joe Campbell, a Riel supporter, a series of grimly comic adventures—finally with the corpse of Riel—emerges. The following takes place immediately after the hanging:

The brothers of the Orange Lodge, Regina Chapter, were climbing into their wagons, now that the party was over. We came face to face with three of them. Get out of my way! Uncle Joe said. One was slow in getting out of the way. Uncle Joe put his hand all over the man's face and pushed. The back of the man's head hit the hub of a wheel. He lay there. That was all. We kept on going. Nothing happened.

Walking back to town, to help my uncle feel better, I said, Maybe the President will send the bluecoats up here to make them pay for what they did.

Redcoats! Bluecoats! my uncle said, I'm sick of them! The only coats I want to see in this western country is buckskin jackets![7]

Matt Cohen's *Too Bad Galahad* (1972), an unpaged assemblage of short parodies or travesties on the Galahad story, is a very expensively printed hardback—a sort of latter-day gift book, perhaps, with illustrations and typographical illuminations. Variously, Galahad is a knight, space traveller, and schoolteacher, who dies several times during the sequence. Here, he is seen arriving at Camelot:

On that day [454 winters after the Crucifixion] Galahad, son of Lancelot, first appeared at Camelot. He walked up to the table and sat at the forbidden seat. He looked young and perfect and everyone was surprised he wasn't struck dead.

Don't all sit there staring at me, he said. Pass me some supper. Many choose but few are chosen.[8]

Eric Koch's *The Leisure Riots* (1973), subtitled "A Comic Novel," envisions a crisis in 1980 during which American young pensioners, retired from top-level executive positions, are in revolt against leisure activities because they are in fact hopelessly addicted to work. They turn violent, with the result that the narrator—Friederich Bierbaum, ex-Nazi think-tanker who fails to come up with the right solution—abruptly becomes an exile in Canada.

Black humor is apparent, increasingly, in fiction appearing

during the later 1960s and on into the 1970s. Some of it is associated with the anti-Vietnam War movement, other parts of it exist for themselves though often allied to poetry or drama. Tinged with bitterness or even drenched in it, often expressed through irony, with a narrowing distinction between laughter and despair, black humor is employed as a natural tool of social protest, or, alternatively, simply a means of scoring off a world assumed beyond redemption. In varying degrees and contexts, this is the tone in works by recent writers such as Juan Butler, Matt Cohen, or David Lewis Stein, and the work of Mordecai Richler is by no means entirely free of it.

Much very acceptable humor is related even more closely to journalism than to fiction *per se*. This helps explain why an earlier humorist such as Peter McArthur has still a loyal following but no place as yet in literary anthologies, or why names like Pierre Berton, Harry J. Boyle, and Eric Nicol appear cheek by jowl with Earle Birney, Robertson Davies, and W. O. Mitchell in the roster of Leacock Medal winners. "As humorist," says Alec Lucas,

. . . McArthur belongs with Haliburton and Leacock as the best in Canadian literature . . . . His career as professional humorist lasted only a few years, however, for he dropped it to become an adherent and advocate of the simple life. He retained his sense of humor, though, and used it in his writing as a method of coating his didacticism or, more often, as a kind of comic relief to his "message."[9]

If one were to multiply, by a factor of ten, the company of Canadian humorists discussed in this present survey alone, he would come up with a very creditable showing indeed *vis-à-vis* American humor, which is world-famous; and that much enlargement, quantitatively, would be needed to compensate for the difference in populations. Ten each of Haliburton, Duncan, Leacock, Birney, and Davies alone would make fifty, and to name even twenty-five American first-raters would not be altogether easy. With this in mind, should not Canadians be a little less disposed to accept themselves meekly as a set of preternaturally earnest, unsmiling, long-suffering sobersides?

CHAPTER 7

Diversities

What is most impressive about this body of fictions [in the year 1970] is not any particular national quality; it is its rich diversity. Some nationalists demand that Canadian writers create a Canadian literature which will mirror a Canada to us and the world. But these writers are going their own way. Their way is "holy particularization." Each has his own sense of place, time, people, and forces.

—Gordon Roper

MOST Canadians, when they think of themselves in national, cultural terms (which are not necessarily parallel concepts, but do tend to fall together, when pushed), are well aware of themselves as one of several North American minorities. This position is usually clearest to them politically and economically, the obvious comparison being with the United States. But there is also awareness in the arts that the size of Canada's population, relative to her vast geographical potential, is one of the most disproportionate in the world. In the wake of such reflections the modern quest for identity takes on special importance for minorities of all kinds, and yet Canada (like the United States and many other countries) is in itself compounded of minorities. How then, one wonders, can anything like monolithic "identity" really be more than a shadowy goal which, even if attainable, might be undesirable? However national identity comes to be thought of, unless its expression is to be a mere paper windmill of propaganda, it will have to leave room for some form of tension: perpetual conflicts of interests spawning wars and violence and wasting the earth (but presumably productive of rewards to the victors), or agreement after ideological contests within a set of rules enforced by a federated consortium, or what? Any country's identity, at last, meets itself in a mirror on the way to the forum.

The two following chapters illustrate the paradoxical nature of the identity problem in Canadian terms as it relates to recent and current fiction. The two chapters are really one, but their separation may help to show a little more clearly (as in Chapter 6) how much diversity there is among English writers of Canadian fiction, arbitrarily setting aside the most spectacular and (some would say) most dangerous diversity of all: the legacy from colliding imperialist powers in the seventeenth and eighteenth centuries. In Chapter 7 it will become clear how different from each other a group of searchers can appear to be within a single containing concept.

I *Aboriginals: Indians, Eskimos*

North American Indians have been comparatively well known to the world and extensively written about since the seventeenth century. With the rise of the novel two hundred years later, John Richardson's *Wacousta* appeared at the same time as Cooper's Leather-Stocking series, and Indians figure intermittently in romances throughout the nineteenth century. The work of Duncan Campbell Scott, who became closely acquainted with Indian life through his post as a public servant, brings us nearer a time when Canadian aboriginals, Indian or Eskimo (to maintain a distinction more geographical than racial), came to be viewed less distantly. Stories about Eskimos began to appear as early as 1857, when R. M. Ballantyne published *Ungava: a Tale of Eskimo Land*, a companion piece to *The Young Fur-Traders: a Tale of the Far North*, the year previous. Until well into the twentieth century, however, both aboriginal types received comparatively more, and more serious, attention in poetry (including poetic drama) than in fiction.

An indication of shifting attitudes is apparent in Hubert R. Evans's *Mist on the River* (1955), the work of a fisheries officer on the coast of British Columbia. Evans's book explores, compassionately but realistically, the diminishing resistance of old ways to new, a theme which runs far back into North American ethnic experience. A novel written by the ethnologist Marius Barbeau in 1928 and recently reprinted (in 1973) called *The Downfall of Temlaham*, deals likewise with West Coast Indians, of the 1880s. It uses tribal mythology in the story of Kamalmuk, who quarrels with his wife (Sunbeams) over the question of accepting the white man. Temlaham is the Indians' settlement on the river, once strong but at last broken by internal tribal conflict. Barbeau's *Mountain Cloud* (1944) is about mixed marriages: whereas a Scottish fur trader deserts his Indian wife, a French Canadian remains loyal to his. A brief, beautifully rendered study of rapport between whites and Indians appears in Margaret Craven's *I Heard the Owl Call My Name* (1967), relating the closing period in the life of a young priest, Mark, spent among the Kwakiutals. In exchange for some of the real comforts of civilization the Indians can offer Mark their fine sense of humor, their sensitivity to others, and their helpfulness in time of need.

Currently, Peter Such, Rudy Wiebe, and W. O. Mitchell offer substantially similar interpretations of Indian life. Such's *Riverrun* (1973) recreates the last quarter-century of the vanished Beothuk Indians, the first North American aboriginals to encounter Europeans, in Newfoundland. Not long after the beginning of the nineteenth century it was clear that this tribe, which resisted accommodation with the whites, could no longer survive. Such's first novel, *Fallout* (1969), also deals with Indians in a northern Ontario mining community, including a successful mixed marriage.

Rudy Wiebe, who is "strongest, and most convincing when speaking for or through the Indian and Eskimo," as Sandra Esche observes,[1] in *The Temptations of Big Bear* (1973) narrates how Big Bear, a Plains Cree chief, understands that the white man with his professional soldiers and transcontinental "iron road" cannot be displaced; nevertheless, Big Bear becomes part of the rebellion of 1885 and is imprisoned. Dick Harrison sees this novel as moving away from the realistic technique of *Peace Shall Destroy Many* (1964)—Wiebe's study of the erosion of Canadian Mennonite communities by World War II—into discontinuous narrative with an interplay of multiple voices which ". . . resembles the way the lenses of a stereoscope draw the separate two-dimensional aerial photographs into a single three-dimensional illusion. The different viewpoints uncover depth and contour invisible to one, and the 'reality' of the vision is not a compromise between views but a new perception entirely." Another critic, P. L. Surette writing in *The Canadian Fiction Magazine* (Spring 1975), believes that Wiebe's work is restoring stature to the historical novel. Its eclecticism combines "a lament for a lost heroic world with lyric songs of violence and grotesque pain with a celebration of suffering and defeat."[2]

W. O. Mitchell's *The Vanishing Point* (1973) employs as central actor-observer, a teacher and Indian agent Carlyle Sinclair, among the Stony tribe at Paradise Valley, a reserve deep in the Canadian Rockies. Together with the last illness, death, and burial of Old Esau, tribal elder, there is a love story, and tensions created by opposing forces among the whites: fundamentalist religious worship versus Indian dances, faith healing by a frenetic American evangelist versus the dispensing of medicine by Carlyle. The strong pull of the old culture is brought out by a moment of timelessness during the "Prairie Chicken Dance":

Who cared now—who cared now! Only the now remained to them—the now so great that only death or love could greaten it. Greater than pain, stronger than hunger or their images paled with future—dimmed with past. Only the now—pulsing and placeless—now! Song and dancer and watching band were one, under the bruising drum that shattered time and self and all other things that bound them.[3]

What today is most desired—an accommodation between races, belated though it may be—appears in Alan Fry's *Come A Long Journey* (1971). Fry's previous books, *Ranch on the Cariboo* (1962) and *How A People Die* (1971), dealt with, respectively, his own boyhood in the rural West and Indians. *Come A Long Journey* tells the simple story of how a white man and an Indian canoe down the Yukon River, Whitehorse to Dawson, hunting moose and mountain sheep, fishing for sustenance, encountering Indian settlements and former settlements. Gradually they become fast friends, and the white man gains a much-increased respect for Indians and Indian culture. Both races have indeed "come a long journey" to reach such understanding, or even to want to reach it. In Matt Cohen's *Wooden Hunters* (1975), set on a coastal island off British Columbia, the picture of Indians as depraved by white culture is grim enough, but the general effect is dulled by repetitiveness and lack of an interesting plot.

The first novel in English to be published by an Eskimo writer appeared in 1970, a novella called *Harpoon of the Hunter*. The author, Markoosie, who lives at Resolute Bay, N.W.T., and works in and out of the Arctic as a charter pilot, tells the story (set in a time before European contact) of a young Kamik's survival and journey home after his hunting companions are killed fighting a rabid polar bear. When he arrives, he finds only more tragedy awaiting him and makes, deliberately, a choice no longer to survive.

Alexander Knox's *Night of the White Bear* (1971) is a story of hunting and hardship not dissimilar to Markoosie's but in a contemporary setting and with a different ending. Uglik, a sixteen-year-old, leaves employment at an American base in the Arctic ("The Station was a wonderful place but the United States soldiers were made to go there without any women . . . no wonder their behaviour was unaccountable and foolish."[4]) to take his chances in the snow and ice rather than submit to sexual mistreatment. Joining old Joe and his pregnant wife Pakti, he lives a less hectic life until old Joe is mauled by a polar bear which begins stalking them; then the story becomes one of craft and survival. Having proved himself, Uglik debates the wisdom of remaining: "How many would die this winter? There'd be a few more babies, but far more piles of stones. The Old Ways were a trap."[5] Uglik decides to turn south.

James Houston's *The White Dawn* (1971) is by another author with first-hand experience among Eskimos, on Baffin Island for twelve years after World War II, nine of them as Civil Administrator. In this story Eskimo meets white man for the first time, when toward the end of the nineteenth century three survivors from a lost whaling boat suddenly appeared. The strangers lived amicably with their rescuers for a time, but at length there was friction and finally judicial violence—planned executions—when it became clear that "these visitors of ours had taken our food and our women and clothing and had given us nothing in exchange, not even clever songs and stories."[6]

Finally, Rudy Wiebe, in *Where Is The Voice Coming From?* (1974), deals realistically with similar themes, for instance, starvation in an Eskimo camp in the story "Oolulik."

White Eskimo (1972) by Harold Horwood is described by its author as "consciously mythological," relating modern life to the days of the Labrador fur trade, as well as "a deliberate revolt against the anti-hero." Its chief character, Gillingham, "is a *real* hero."[7] Norah Story sees in the story something other than simon-pure heroism, however, remarking: "Unfortunately Horwood echoes the propaganda of many of the St. John's fur-trade and merchant interests against the work of the Moravian missions and the International Grenfell Foundation—work that is too well documented to be denigrated."[8]

Through most of these writers there runs a strong current of concern with the past, either as a record of social error or as the source of story-plots. We have observed this already in historical fiction—by William Kirby, W. R. Bird, and Thomas Raddall, for example—and find it here still operating. In the fiction of Robert Harlow (b. 1923) the past is all but overpowering: *Royal Murdoch* (1962) shows us the influence of a pioneer over the town he settled, long past his death; in *A Gift of Echoes* (1965) the hero attempts to find identity through reenacting the past; and in *Scann* (1972) the title character, a newspaper man, is likewise fascinated with interpreting historical influence through a chronicle of British Columbia town life from 1910 through 1960.

II · Migrants and Immigrants

The previous chapter has already shown us that lonely Irish immigrants in Montreal were handled, a generation ago, with sympathy and skill in the fiction of Jessie Sime. So pervasive is the immigrant motif in Canada, and indeed all North America, that a separate volume would be needed to treat it fully. The Maritime Provinces received thousands of Loyalists after the American Revolution. Early in the nineteenth century settlers came to both Upper and Lower Canada from the British Isles, and after mid-century the Canadian prairies began to be populated by thousands of first-generation settlers from continental Europe: Grove, the earliest prairie novelist of stature, was one of them. In our own time, immigration flows principally to urban areas, on both coasts. As we look at the fictional product of later-type immigration and internal movement, we become gradually aware that in Canada, as elsewhere, the novel in English has already grown international in many aspects, not least in the stories associated with international migration—some of it (from the Caribbean, for instance) of quite recent origin. In this section we shall meet the veteran chronicler of Irish-Canadians, Brian Moore, along with the gypsy novelist Ronald Lee and two writers, Austin Clarke and Frederick Ward, who deal with black immigrant experience.

Brian Moore began writing and publishing in Belfast, where he grew up. Upon coming to Canada in 1948 he naturally did not begin immediately to draw upon Canadian experience; the Irish heritage still governed his work. But by 1956 he had published *Judith Hearne*, a sensitive portrayal of a lonely shy, plain spinster who in her forties, having been brought up in the Catholic Ulster tradition in Belfast, begins to descend into alcoholism. Here we encounter her talking to her priest:

> "Father," the woman said, beginning to weep, "Father, I'm all alone. I need somebody."
> She bent over. Her red hat fell off, rolled on the floor. Father Quigley picked it up.
> "I need a sign," the woman said. "I need a sign from God."
> "You need to sober up, that's what you need."
> "But Father, I'm not—not drunk, now. Honestly, Father, I can't believe any more. I can't pray. He won't listen. Maybe it's the devil tempting me as you said, Father, but I just don't feel that God is there any more. Nobody is listening. All my life I've believed, I've waited—Father, listen to me!"
> "I'm listening," Father Quigley said grimly.
> "Father, why is it? You're a priest. Are *you* sure He's there? Are you really sure?"[9]

In *The Feast of Lupercal* (1957), also set in Belfast, Moore undertook a somewhat Joyce-like portrait of Diarmuid Devine, English teacher at an authoritarian Catholic boys' school. Three years later came *The Luck of Ginger Coffee* (1960), which marks Moore's final commitment to the New World. Hallvard Dahlie describes the transition in these terms:

> The direction in Moore's fiction has clearly been towards a progressive emancipation of his characters: from *Judith Hearne* and *Lupercal* with their characters locked in the stifling environment of Belfast, to *Ginger Coffee* and *Limbo* with their immigrant characters caught up in the flux and uncertainties, but also the possibilities of the New World, and finally to *Emperor* and *Mary Dunne*, whose protagonists are triumphant and emancipated.[10]

Thus, *Ginger Coffee* is not only a study in the assimilation of an Irish immigrant to the realities (and solemnities) of Montreal society; it is proof, as well, of a writer's ability to make a similar transition, as many others had done before him all the way back to Susanna Moodie or even earlier. Ginger's "luck" is more bad than good throughout most of the book: he is either unemployed (not "poor in spirit"— "just poor") or else working at jobs not suited to his abilities, and he has serious domestic problems. At the end, however, things begin to look brighter. Moore's ability to portray, realistically and with color and humor, lower middle class daily life is abundantly evident throughout. At the end of it all, "Didn't most men try and fail, weren't most men losers? Didn't damn nearly everyone have to face up some day to the fact that their ship would never come in?"[11] But this is not quite Ginger's final mood, or word: "Going on was the victory"—success was strangely dissolved in life itself.

This novel rejects over-facile generalities about Canada and indeed the whole New World, as for instance when Ginger watches, or tries to watch, a film in which

. . . somehow the filmed America no longer seemed true. He could not believe in this America, this land that half the world dreams of in dark front seats in cities and villages half a world away. What had it in common with his true America? For Canada was America; the difference a geographer's line. What had the Hollywood revels to do with the facts of life in a cold New World?[12]

And later, at a "Five Minute Lunch" bar,

"He didn't want to talk about Canada," Fox said. "Leave Canada out. There you have the Canadian dilemma in a sentence. Nobody wants to talk about Canada, not even us Canadians. You're right, Paddy. Canada is a bore."

Paddy (i.e., Ginger) has been misunderstood, but that gives Fox an opportunity to indulge in a fairly common Canadian indoor sport.[13]

Moore's *I Am Mary Dunne* (1968) presents a thrice-married woman who, beginning to doubt her identity, relives her marriages.

And what are these dooms of mine [she asks herself] but a frightening, unreal play going on inside my head, a play I must sit through and suffer, for if I do not fight them, the dooms will not leave me.[14]

The Revolution Script (1971) chronicles the lurid events of October 1970 (the "October Crisis") when the Front de Liberation du Quebec kidnapped the British Trade Commissioner, James Cross (later released), and murdered Pierre Laporte, Quebec Minister of Labor and Immigration. *Fergus* (1970) and *The Great Victorian*

Collection (1975) are treated in Chapter 7 under "Fantasy and Parable."

Austin Clarke is an immigrant writer from Barbados who, like Moore, uses in his early work the characters and setting of his homeland. The first two titles, *The Survivors of the Crossing* (1964) and *Amongst Thistles and Thorns* (1965) in themselves imply problems. In *The Meeting Point* (1967) there is a three-part division (Clarke himself thinks of it as having symphonic-like divisions): 1) The Experience of Arrival, in which sister Estelle arrives from Barbados to visit Bernice Leach, maid for a well-to-do Jewish couple in Toronto; 2) The Taste of the Apple; and 3) The Triangle is Smashed—problems again, sexual and otherwise, in the second and third parts. This book offers authentic West Indian dialogue and a lively sense of incident as does the next, *When He Was Free and Young and He Used to Wear Silks* (1971), a story-collection. Of the latter, Margaret Atwood says:

You might expect the stories to be about black-white relationships, and there is a little of this, but the real core of the book seems to be money: the difficulty of obtaining it, the consequences of not having it, the resentment against others who have it—especially European immigrants—and the spiritual price paid by those who get it and their ultimate failure anyway.[15]

Clarke, says Norah Story, is "too good a writer to stop short at bitterness. His writing is leavened by humor, compassion, and generosity of spirit; his scenes and the idiosyncrasies of his characters are full of life."[16]

Riverlisp (1974) by Frederick Ward is written in rhythmical, often poetic prose—"to be read with indulgence . . . out loud," as the flyleaf suggests—developing a number of black characters in "Riverlisp," a town that represents numerous black settlements the author recalls from both Canada and the United States. The Canadian one most closely associated with him is Africville, on the outskirts of Halifax, which had undergone "redevelopment" by the time he took up residence there in 1970. This passage offers a clue as to style and content:

Juka tol one time O they neighborhood was a fashionable part of town and as everyone was worried bout the safety and protection of the area (our care was in taxes) plicemens in helicopters with search lights

patroled at night, occasionally lightening up suspicious shadows. Black
peopled never faired well in that neighborhood.[17]

One of the world's oldest and most widely spread group of
migrants appears in *Goddam Gypsy* (1971) by Ronald Lee. The
author explains that the episodes are autobiographical "in places
fictionalized, a parallel rather than the actuality," and in the
foreword he says: "We are the world's oldest living non-
conformists. Are we also the world's last?" No small part of the
problem is revealed in this bit of dialogue:

> Jimmy and I had one last drink in the house. I took my glass and threw
> it against the wall where it smashed into fragments.
> "To hell with Canada, Long live Romanestan."
> Jimmy looked at me, only half understanding. He had heard of the
> proposed Gypsy state, a parallel to Israel, to be set up by the United
> Nations at the insistence of Gypsy leaders in Europe, educated men like
> me, who had found that they had no place as Romanies in their countries
> of birth. But it meant little to Jimmy. His main trouble was finding
> enough to eat and to keep his instruments and amplifier in shape.[18]

III   *Canadian Jewish Fiction*

For centuries Jews have been, par excellence, migrants and
immigrants; so Canadian Jewish fiction is in effect an extension of
the topic just discussed. The reason for giving it separate treatment is not only that there is so much of it, but that so much of it is
of high quality. Moreover, as the literary historian W. H. New
points out, one of the things demonstrated by the series of novels
detailing Jewish experience in Canada is that the "realistic" mode
of fiction did not die in the 1960s.

But for the most part it became the domain of the ethnic minorities. Such
novels mirrored directly the "newspaper" realities of physical labour, sex,
poverty, crime and hunger; whatever the abstract topics they broached,
their concern was to record that which was seen and heard in "ordinary"
neighbourhoods rather than that which was dreamed or imagined. The
concern for the "ordinary" was a testament to their social commitment.[19]

This section does not bring together all the Jewish writers included
in this book (several appear, for example, in Chapter 7) but it does
illustrate the range of their work, from earnest protest against

local anti-Semitism and European persecution to satire against Jews from within their own race.

Earth and High Heaven by Gwethalyn Graham was published in 1944, using the background of Montreal during World War II to portray anti-Semitic attitudes on the part of a well-to-do Gentile family, the Drakes. When their daughter Erica meets and falls in love with Marc Reiser, an intelligent young Jewish lawyer from a small town, the Drakes set about destroying the relationship. What they succeed in doing is destroying their relationship with Erica, and the parting exchange between father and daughter is conducted in these acrimonious terms:

"You got what you wanted," she said, paying no attention. "He isn't going to marry a Drake. You fixed it." She went a little closer to him and asked, "Would you like to know how you fixed it, Charles?"

"Erica, I warn you I'm not going to stand for much more of this. . . ."

"Oh, now look," said Erica, "be reasonable. For almost three months you've been saying exactly what you liked and writing it all off under the heading of Father Knows Best. I'm not going to take three months, I'll probably be finished in less than three minutes. That's fair enough, isn't it?" . . . [She is as good as her word; then, finally]:

He said, peering at her, his voice hardly more than a whisper, "You are going, Erica?"

"Yes, I'm going," said Erica. "And I'm not coming back again."[20]

Tension, tragedies, and differences in the Jewish community itself, both in Canada and Europe, are also evident in the fiction of four writers whose material relates closely to Jewish tradition, particularly with a view toward revealing the crises relating to World War II. The first novel, Henry Kreisel's *The Rich Man* (1952), sends a Canadian immigrant, Jacob, back to Vienna where his relatives find it hard to believe that he is in fact not a rich man although his children have done well for themselves and he does not (in 1935) have to face the threat of Hitler. In this scene (which occurs more than once, since Jacob's relatives—partly with his own unconscious encouragement—believe he is, like nearly all Americans, abundantly rich) Jacob is being approached with a bona fide appeal for help:

"Yankel," he [Reuben] said softly, imploringly, "help Shaendl. To you four thousand schillings must be like nothing. If you give it to Shaendl, you will have plenty left for yourself, and you will do one of the greatest

things a man can do in this world, to help a widow and her children . . . .
Yankel, for the sake of your father (may he rest in peace) and for the sake
of your mother, help your sister Shaendl."

What shall I tell him? God, what shall I tell him? What will he say
when he knows the truth? What will Manya say? How will they look at
me when I tell them? And my mother, and Shaendl, what will they say?
Will they believe me? Will they believe me when I tell them?[21]

In *The Second Scroll* (1951) by A. M. Klein the Holocaust has
already taken place and Israel has emerged as a new nation. The
book is both prose and verse, with about two-thirds of the total
related by the nephew of Melech Davidson who after the war goes
in search of his uncle but arrives too late to meet him alive. In the
following passage, the nephew, just arrived in Israel, enters a
synagogue where he finds an old man and a young boy studying
the Scriptures together.

They affirmed it for me, the young boy prodigy and the old man who
looked like Elijah: Israel had not only returned back into Time; it still
belonged to Eternity.

I hesitated to break upon their studies; but soon the elder, sensing my
presence, rose from his bench to greet me . . . . Our conversation was in
Yiddish, for the old man was of those who held that Hebrew would be
profaned by secular use.

"From where comes a Jew?" he asked.

"From Canada."

"Canada!" He sucked at his gums. "A great distance!"

"I flew. With the aeroplane it is not so great a distance."

"True . . . . True. We live in Messiah's days."

"Because the world is all good? Or, *cholila*, all evil?"

"Judgements are for God. . . ."[22]

Klein, says A. M. Steinberg, "in this novel accepts the traditional
Jewish position"—conceiving of reason and will as expanding and
evolving under divine law. He adds, "*The Second Scroll*, however,
is a religious novel in an even more fundamental and universal
sense. The universality of Klein's religious theme is made evident
by his indicating the essential oneness of the three major western
religions: Judaism, Christianity, and Mohammedanism."[23]

Much of the expanded religious element is developed in a
number of "glosses" in lyric verse. On the language of the novel,
Miriam Waddington writes:

Klein's diction combined the vocabulary, syntax, and idiom of at least three languages. Klein's syntactical structures, when they are not English, are most often Hebrew; his idiom is Yiddish, translated with a fanatical literalness, which is in contrast with the way he translates Yiddish poetry. His linguistic style and word consciousness are Joycean.[24]

Michael Jacot in *The Last Butterfly* (1973) offers a chronicle of Jewish life in a Czechoslovakian concentration camp. (The title comes from a child's poem stating that butterflies don't live in the ghetto.) No one is spared, Jew or German or Czech alike; the book is a testimony of the ultimate degradations to which humanity can sink, a no-hope record of terrorism and death. Finally, Adele Wiseman in *The Sacrifice* (1956) and *Crackpot* (1974) deals again with immigrants to Canada. *The Sacrifice* uses the framework of the Abraham-Isaac story to develop a conflict in a modern Abraham, who having lost two of his three sons in Europe, becomes embittered and finally in a crazed compulsion for sacrifice kills an elderly woman and is confined in an asylum, Mad Mountain. His grandson, Moses, goes to visit him—unwillingly, since he has grown up feeling repelled by what he thinks his grandfather must be—and during their encounter they reach an understanding that in some strange fashion transmutes hatred into love. About this novel Margaret Atwood writes:

> Even though its protagonist ends his days as an insane murderer, *The Sacrifice* closes on a relatively positive note, with the generations reconciled and a future of possibilities made available to the grandson. Wiseman can only project authentic success into the future, not depict it; but the chief obstacles to success—rejecting the new land altogether, and being destructively assimilated by it—do seem to have been effectively worked through in the first two generations. Imagining success for the grandson does not seem—in the book's terms—unrealistic.[25]

Crackpot is the extensive chronicle of Hoda who, coming as a child to Winnipeg, remains there as a prostitute and mothers a child of her own, through whom her world gradually expands. Other women writers on Jewish life include Charlotte Fielden with *Crying As She Ran* (1970), Phyllis Gotlieb with *Why Should I Have All the Grief?* (1969), and Hilda Shubert with *They Came from Kernitz* (1969).

Norman Levine, who deals less exclusively with Jewish character, in his stories and novels sees himself as twice-fugitive in that at

McGill, where he began *The Angled Road* (1952), he was "running away from Canada," giving his stories of Canadian life English settings. Until *Canada Made Me* (1958), from which he dates his mature work, he seemed to feel a "sense of paleness and unreality."²⁶ His very humble background in Ottawa is recalled in "A Father" and highlighted again in "In Quebec City," both stories from a recent collection, *I Don't Want to Know Anyone Too Well* (1970). Levine's natural affinity for people, coupled with a somewhat nostalgic temperament, appears to advantage in *From A Seaside Town* (1970) in which the narrator, a travel-journalist, is left on his own resources by a magazine's failure. Gradually, as time passes, he begins to see life for its own sake, and for his sake as well, instead of something to be treated objectively, professionally. Levine's fiction, in broad terms, contains rather less angst than that of most of his Jewish-Canadian contemporaries.

A transition from Levine to Mordecai Richler can be made through *We Always Take Care of Our Own* (1965) by C. J. Newman, a humorous account of what happens when Meyer Rabinovitch, a rebellious young man (normal enough for the 1960s), becomes a beggar to disprove the adage that there are no Jewish beggars. Richler's approach to Jewish character (already suggested in Chapter 5) began in earnest with *Son of a Smaller Hero* (1955), a fictional autobiography about the Jewish community in Montreal, and reached full stature in *The Apprenticeship of Duddy Kravitz* (1959), his best known work and "one of the richest of contemporary Canadian novels."²⁷ A film version of this novel has been made. Not untypically, Duddy grows up amid ghetto surroundings in Montreal. Here, his relationships to both the Anglo-Saxon and French-Canadian communities are not surprisingly ambivalent in such a divided city. Richler creates characters in prodigal abundance with whom Duddy interacts. He remains loyal to his family and ethnic origins, despite harsh things that are said about the overpossessiveness of Jewish motherhood, the sentimentality behind Zionism, and the difficulties within the family which breed in Duddy his "potentially violent emotions [which] illustrate Richler's view of the Jewish family as a psychological pressure cooker."²⁸ Duddy's emotions and his evident business abilities find an outlet when he plans to turn a mountain lake area into a haven for Jews. We are left wondering: can this be adequate for him? What *does* Duddy actually represent? Varying critical interpretations have left ample room for the reader to draw his own conclusions, but there is not much doubt concerning Richler's determined use of a fascinating Jewish character and of Jewishness itself to explore ideas lying beyond either one *per se.* The critic John Ower concludes:

> While an understanding of Duddy's ethnic background is necessary for a full comprehension of his "apprenticeship," his career is placed in a broader human context through Richler's satiric vision. In this regard, Duddy becomes a vehicle for conveying a complex ironic outlook by which a number of different perspectives are partially condemned and by which most of Richler's characters are shown as having both their good points and their shortcomings. In particular, Duddy indicates that his creator has like many satirists a jaundiced view of human nature and little faith in its improvability. To some extent, Duddy represents (and also becomes increasingly aware of) the incurable evil and sickness of man and his society, a nastiness which must be faced, if we are to be at all realistic and honest, and coped with if we are to survive.[29]

Richler's incisive social comment is to be found also in David Lewis Stein. *Scratch One Dreamer* (1967) portrays a soured personal relationship within the family, and in *My Sexual and other Revolutions* (1971) the "treatment of sex is overpowering and includes aberrations. Stein can foresee only anarchy followed by tyranny for the world he portrays."[30]

IV *Diversity in Canadian Short Fiction*

The earliest raconteurs in Canada were the Indians and Eskimos, many of whose stories have been recorded. Short fiction, some of it written deliberately for magazine publication, existed in some quantity early in the nineteenth century: Mrs. Moodie, McCulloch, and Haliburton were basically writers of descriptive narratives and character sketches lightly tied together. Later in the century Parker began his career in much the same fashion; and such notables as Leacock, Edward William Thomson, D.C. Scott, Nellie McClung, Peter McArthur, and Charles G.D. Roberts (famous for animal stories, as have been other Canadians—e.g. Ernest Thompson Seton and Roderick Haig–Brown) were storytellers in addition to having other literary talents. The prairie stories of Grove and Knister were well-known predecessors of later ones by Sinclair Ross and Margaret Laurence, to whose names may be added those of Ethel Wilson, Howard O'Hagan, Hugh Garner, and Morley Callaghan.

When in 1968 Hugh Garner, writing a foreword for Alice Munro's *Dance of the Happy Shades*, drew up his short list of those he considered the good Canadian short-story writers, the "real ones," he named Alice Munro, Ethel Wilson, Morley Callaghan, W. O. Mitchell, Brian Moore, Margaret Laurence, Mordecai Richler, Ernest Buckler, "and about as many more as can be counted on Lord Nelson's fingertips," speaking of the younger generation rather unhopefully:

> While hardly any of the new writers have learned how to write a classic short story—or any type of short story at all—many of them are getting into print writing illiterate 150-page so-called "novels," which are anything but. They are hippy revelations of their personal hang-ups, their juvenile autobiographies and their startling—to them—discoveries of sex. This trend will kill the novel just as the formula story killed that branch of literature.[31]

Another list, compiled a few years later, naming the "chief prose writers" of the 1960s, yields the following: Margaret Atwood, Clark Blaise, Matt Cohen, A. J. Elliott, Mavis Gallant, Hugh Garner, Dave Godfrey, David Helwig, Hugh Hood, Margaret Laurence, Norman Levine, Malcolm Lowry, Gwendolyn Mac-Ewen, John Metcalf, Alice Munro, C. J. Newman, Alden Nowlan, Mordecai Richler, Jane Rule, Ray Smith, Audrey Thomas, Rudy Wiebe—rather clearly the compilation of a younger critic.[32] A mixture from both lists is to be encountered in Norman Levine's anthology, *Canadian Winter's Tales* (1968): Morley Callaghan, Mavis Gallant, Hugh Hood, Margaret Laurence, Norman Levine, Malcolm Lowry, Brian Moore, Mordecai Richler, Ethel Wilson. Perhaps something like a consensus is beginning to take shape.

Earlier in the 1960s, Klinck's *Literary History of Canada* reported a "decline in the prestige of the short story . . . so marked, in fact, that it must be recognized as symptomatic of a radically changed literary situation."[33] Another fifteen years, however, saw the establishment of *Canadian Fiction*, *Prism International*, and many more periodicals hospitable to the form; and the appearance of not just one or two but a large group of talented new writers tended to dispel the gloom of the early prediction. The short story, like the poem, turned out to be a good probe for searchers. Moreover, the Canadian Broadcasting Corporation continued to support story-writers; it is common to find acknowledgments such as the one from Levine's *I Don't Want to Know Anyone Too Well*: "Six of the stories have been read over the C. B. C. program 'Anthology.'" By 1974, then, the editors of a fourth annual collection, *74: New Canadian Stories*, could say with confidence: "In the last four years, we have published 50 stories by 39 writers. Now and then a reviewer announces that the short story is dead, but we aren't convinced. Here is part of our evidence."[34]

Conditions were ripe, as well, for experimentation with technique. Social realism—with or without hippy dialogue, embellishments, and other special devices—is to be found chiefly among the "consensus" writers listed above. And so even-paced a writer as Alice Munro is not above occasional innovation deliberately calling attention to technique. Her story "Home," in the 1974 collection just mentioned, takes the narrator back to her rural home on a series of three buses symbolic of systematic withdrawal from the city. Arriving, she finds her much-loved father living with a pert stepmother the narrator cannot warm up to. At the end of the story the father contracts heart trouble and is not receiving very expert treatment. Interspersed throughout the story are notes in italics describing the narrator's difficulties with presentation, with a long one at the close beginning *"I don't know how to end this"* and commenting further on the narrator's problems as narrator. To some readers, no doubt, a device like this would seem a bit too self-conscious, but it is symptomatic of a widespread desire among writers to ventilate the form by "making it new." And the critical response to not a few of the writers was frequently the same as that to Lawrence Garber's three stories in *Circuit* (1970): "brilliantly written: inventive in image, taut with energy, and relentless in building nauseous effects."[35]

V   A Gathering: Twenty-Two Recent Titles in Canadian Short Fiction

Within the stated purpose of revealing diversity, this long paragraph takes twenty-two recent authors, with one book-title for each, offering the briefest of comment to identify and/or characterize the work:

Will R. Bird, *Angel Cove*, 1972: Newfoundland coastal towns in pre-confederation years, with stress on the hardships of seafaring life, by a veteran story-writer.

Clark Blaise, *A North American Education*, 1973: more or less autobiographical, relating the narrator's efforts to adapt to too-rapid changes; sensitive to small concrete details and engagingly written.

Max Braithwaite, *Never Sleep Three in a Bed*, 1969: hardscrabble youth in the prairie country, related with humorous recollection.

Harry Bullock, *Green Beginning: Black Ending*, 1971: varied themes, with surrealistic treatment.

Austin Clarke, *When He Was Free and Young and He Used to Wear Silks*, 1971: semi-impressionistic work using West Indian immigrant experiences.

Matt Cohen, *Too Bad, Galahad*, 1973: pseudo-cycle of humorous-ironic sketches commingling medieval and modern; printed and embellished as an album-type book.

Mavis Gallant, *The Pegnitz Junction*, 1973: about German characters, both at home and abroad, by an author with long European residence.

Dave Godfrey, *Death Goes Better with Coca Cola*, 1967: sport stories of hunting and fishing, examining the cruelty involved; critical of the Canadian ethos.

David Helwig, *The Streets of Summer*, 1969: various situations and settings, including hippy Toronto, handled with skill.

Margaret Laurence, *A Bird in the House*, 1970: part of the author's "Manawaka" world—stories centering in the growth and maturation, not without friction and sorrow, of the narrator-heroine Vanessa MacLeod.

Norman Levine, *I Don't Want to Know Anyone Too Well*, 1971: set variously in England and Canada; carefully constructed and well-finished.

Gwendolyn MacEwen, *Noman*, 1972: deeply immersed in dream-sequence experiences and the occult.

Joyce Marshall, *A Private Place*, 1975: stress on the psychology of girls and women, in Canadian and foreign settings.

John Metcalf, *The Lady Who Sold Furniture*, 1970: novella and stories mostly in British settings, ranging from childhood to old age.

Alice Munro, *Lives of Girls and Women*, 1971: semi-novel sequence using an observer-narrator's experiences with mother and family, friends, school.

Alden Nowlan, *Miracle at Indian River*, 1968: in New Brunswick settings; episodes revealing the limitations of small-town life in the Maritimes.

Andreas Schroeder, *The Late Man*, 1972: predominantly fantasy and symbolism, with techniques influenced by painting and film-making.

Ray Smith, *Cape Breton is the Thought Control Centre of Canada*, 1969: humor in "combined fiction," or skits and take-offs on less boisterous writers.

Vasyl Stefanyk, *The Stone Cross*, 1971: English translation of stories by the Ukrainian immigrant writer Stefanyk (1876-1935) showing early immigrant experience in the Canadian west.

Merna Summers, *The Skating Party*, 1974: farm stories—e.g., "The Blizzard"—from the viewpoint of a young girl; somewhat of a recent counterpart to Knister, perhaps, but more objective.

Audrey Thomas, *Ten Green Bottles*, 1967: childhood; adult womanhood; race prejudice in Africa, mostly in sombre tones.

W.D. Valgardson, *God Is Not a Fish Inspector*, 1975: Manitoba life presented in strident language, amid a general aura of selfishness resulting in cheating, adultery, murder, and suicide.

CHAPTER 8

Searchers

In Canada today there is practically no cultural pressure on the novelist: he has something nearer absolute freedom in subject and form than he has ever had.

—Donald Cameron

IT IS commonplace, by now, to say that we are well into some variety or other of neoromanticism, with which critics will be busy most likely for the rest of the century. Along with European, American, and all other writers of English, younger Canadian novelists reflect this tendency in addition to helping sustain it. Their fiction—especially the "search for identity" variety—is involved with it in all sorts of ways, as shown by numerous interviews with authors broadcast by the CBC and later published as collections. One who wishes to understand (or try to understand) what the current aims in Canadian fiction really are should read liberally in these interviews, especially of authors born no earlier than the 1930s: at a venture, Austin Clarke (from Barbados) whose phrase "vindictively ritualistic" thoroughly sums up a great deal of the protest literature; Marian Engel, who thinks that "It's very Canadian to be hung up on morals"; Dave Godfrey, who "actually . . . started out to be three things, a musician, an engineer, and a writer"; Alice Munro, who thinks that men "assume their pursuits are more important and their gifts too, probably"; Scott Symons, a professing mystic but critically very acute in assessing the Canadian literary world; and Rudy Wiebe, from the prairie country, deeply engaged with the symbiotic relations of history and myth.

Readers and listeners may learn, then, that contemporary Canadian novelists—the majority, though not all—show a profound disturbance about the state of their world. This may take the form of psychological studies (especially of women, both old and young), social satires, or fantasies. Some of the protest is directed at the United States, some of it at the divisions within Canadian life for which the mechanistic, money-ridden culture below the border, as it is widely viewed above the border, cannot be fairly blamed. By no means are all such divisions linguistic or economic; authors feel themselves, for all their remarkable achievements of the past fifteen to twenty-five years, neglected— so much so that the gap between artist and public appears as "the crucial problem of the Canadian tradition, from a perspective within," as John Moss has recently expressed it.

A thriving literature is largely devoid of appreciation, despite occasional garlands of "Canlit" scattered among the curricula of our academies. Art unread withers in vision; a people unread in visions of themselves wither in imagination and sensibility. Unless the Canadian literary tradition takes hold in the educated imagination of the community which generates it, and thence takes its place in a dynamic consortium of world literature, that is our future.[1]

It should be added that such anxiety is by no means peculiar to Canadian writers (though they have talked about it incessantly for quite a long time); New Zealanders feel it at least as acutely, if not more so, as do West Indians, Africans, and more than a few Americans.

Within this same context it is tempting though not always entirely fair-minded to assume that all the fault lies with the readership. Hasn't the artist done his part by producing his stories, poems, plays? Isn't it obvious that a public that refuses to read them must be unsympathetic, unreflective, stupid? Perhaps so, but one needs to ask, as well, whether the artist's choices of means are always within the grasp of his audience: does he really understand his audience as well as he ought to and needs to? Can the writer ever be too esoteric, too uncompromisingly angry and sarcastic or too arcanely symbolic, or too far upstage in some other respect?

Nor is all the tension just between writer and audience. Writers and critics alike are sometimes disturbed by the contemporary literary scene, or at any rate by some of its most extremely "romantic" manifestations. Donald Cameron sees as pervasive "The Bizarre and the Freaky in Recent Canadian Literature" (title of an essay published in 1974). W. H. New, summarizing the uncertain mood of the 1960s, points out that even in the popular-formula novel, instead of customary saccharine solutions, there is "an accompanying kind of muted terror."

This perhaps has always been true, from Gothic novels to detective fiction, and so it is not surprising to find it in Arthur Hailey's *In High Places* (1961), Charles Israel's *The Hostages* (1966), or in other works by these prolific writers.[2]

The example cited in which such terror is the dominant note is James Clavell's *King Rat* (1962). Somewhat later, by the early 1970s, New observed that

. . . simple linear narrative was giving way to complex artifice; "realism" was losing ground to improvisational modes, to science fiction, to the surreal, the absurd, and the consciously contrived mythic and fabular; ethnic minorities sounded their various voices; cultural nationalism took the place of liberal internationalism; political and social pressures were resulting in literary commitments to moral choice, although such choice was frequently predicated on a rejection of institutional mores; and a remarkable amount of good writing appeared.[3]

Kent Thompson, writing in *Fiddlehead* (March-April 1970), lays part of the blame on pressures for novelty:

We live in the age of "developments of literature" . . . and the serious writer is expected to push away at the bounds of literary conventions. In short, he must take a flashy splash.

   For too many years this has meant that young writers have imitated James Joyce and have quite blithely forgotten that he was born in the 19th century and died well before the mid-point of this one. Now they imitate Leonard Cohen's *Beautiful Lovers*, or Beckett, or William Burroughs, Henry Miller, etc., etc. The complete provincialism of this kind of imitation seems to have bothered no one at all.[4]

About the same judgment will at last be made, most probably, of Canadian novelists as of American ones who took the "counter-culture" revolution of the 1960s, with its sexual liberations, as warrant for interminable saturnalia of the genitalia. What Dr. Johnson said (not very sympathetically) of Thomas Gray applies to some of the more effusive recent works more truly now than to Gray's two hundred years ago: "He was dull in a new way, and that made many people think him great." When one reads

enough, or perchance too many, of these stories and novels
(Canadian or otherwise) in tight sequence, all the clanging,
hammering, wheezing, maundering, and caterwauling tend to
converge at last into a kind of "white noise," still of considerable
intensity though very low in interest. Not to suggest however, that
degeneration, doom, and destruction are all that Canadian novelists can now ever think of, a final footnote may be added citing the
novel *Knowledge Park* (1972) by Stephen Franklin, which sees
Canada by the year 2000 as no longer under American domination
but, instead, ready to undertake building the largest library in the
world as a gesture toward stability and security on the world
scale.

Possibly by the mid-1970s the flow had begun to subside, if the
words of a second contributor to *Fiddlehead* (Winter 1976) can be
taken as a directional sign:

> A peculiar feature of the novel's excessive literary style is its use of sex,
> excretion, and violence. [It] clearly asks us to gorge ourselves to the point
> of sickness and nausea, but I, for one, prefer plainer, more homely fare.[5]

It could be argued that what the reviewer objects to *is* plain and
homely, but the larger implication may be that, sooner or later, a
point is reached where *everyone* tires of the perpetual peep show.
Hugh MacLennan is one who thinks so. "I can't believe," he says,
referring to the products of the 1960s especially, "that this present
tide of pornography, self-hatred, self-contempt and boring drug-
fed egoism can last indefinitely, or even much longer, and this I
infer from the tastes of my students."[6]

This chapter offers, first—as establishing a more or less general
contemporary tone—a quick excursion through a number of titles
published in the early 1970s. Next, it turns to authors who deal
with some of the topics common to recent fiction: personal and
social demoralization, the feminist movement, academic life,
fantasy and parable, and questionings of the form and purposes of
fiction itself. Finally there is a brief summing-up, and a conclusion to the entire work.

I *Sampler-Spectrum, 1970–73*

The ten novels capsulized below are identified at the end of the
section. As a group they reveal, concentrated within a short space

of time—the early 1970s—a number of the themes and techniques of special interest to novelists within the past few years.

1) A murderer unburdens himself to a doctor in a mental hospital. After a long account, delivered in a lean, sardonic, impressive style, the speaker turns upon his listener and demands:

> You tell me something now. I've told you enough. How can such sickness exist in the world? Surely the choice is obvious: either we exterminate it, stamp on it, smash every sign of it, or else we leave it as it is; and if we do this we're admitting complicity in the whole mess. Worse than that, we're saying that we're part of it. Non-playing members, maybe, but members all the same.[7]

2) Jake Martens goes to London to find his brother John, of the Canadian foreign service, who has been implicated in espionage.

3) The story recreates the court life of Pharoah Akhenaton, his queen Nefertiti, and his militant monotheism which brought him his ruin.

4) A "mixed media" pair: the first uses journal-like narrative back-to-back with concrete poetry forms and cartoonlike illustrations (in color) and other drawings; the second (its title is derived from Christopher Smart's "Jubilato Agno") is principally erotic fantasy, with no drawings but a good many blank or partly blank pages.

5) A pretended "documentary" which turns out to be a travesty of *The Tempest:* the documents are papers, tapes, filmstrips, diaries, letters, and photographs, discovered by a Dr. Anthrax Teitlebaum (of the British Museum) in the Scrod Hotel, Vancouver—chiefly one more "dam-buster" romp through various forms of sexuality.

6) A "fictional memoir" in which stories are loosely carpentered into a novel whose narrator, to quote his own metaphor, is a bit too much "caught inside his own skull like a lightning bug in a jam jar."

7) William Boyd, a retired American teacher, buys a duplex in Fredericton and begins becoming a Canadian and a writer (of an "Alien's Guide to Survival"); however, once he has rented the other half of the duplex to Corrie and Tennie he begins fantasizing about them, and. . . .

8) A montage-like presentation of a wedding reception at which all is not sweet, all is not sound.

9) Freddy Landon of Toronto, middle-aged and alone, begins to find some peace and comfort through the friendship of a spinster schoolteacher who lives in the same apartment block, when his estranged wife and daughter abruptly reappear and add complications. Driving through the cold in his ancient De Soto, Freddy becomes extremely uncomfortable, and reflects:

> Something was wrong with the heater, and by turns it blew great blasts of hot and cold air over Landon's crotch. There was much to repair in the old car. In his life too. There were many questions that needed answers.[8]

10) A satirical account of what Hollywood does to its writers.

Identifications

1. Michael Charters, *Victor Victim*, 1970.
2. David Helwig, *The Day Before Tomorrow*, 1971.
3. Gwendolyn McEwen, *King of Egypt, King of Dreams*, 1971.
4. B. P. Nichol, *Two Novels: Andy* and *For Jesus Lunatick*, 1971.
5. John Mills, *The Land of Is.* 1972.
6. Alden Nowlan, *Various Persons Named Kevin O'Brien*, 1973.
7. Kent Thompson, *The Tenants Were Corrie and Tennie*, 1973.
8. Helen Weinzweig, *In Passing Ceremony*, 1973.
9. Richard B. Wright, *In the Middle of a Life*, 1973.
10. Rachel Wyatt, *The String Box*, 1970.

II *Personal and Social Demoralization*

Cult figures of our time have included, in British/American literature, Dylan Thomas, Ernest Hemingway, and Jack Kerouac, to name a trio familiar to all. Much the same function has been performed for Canadian literature through fiction by an expatriate Englishman, Malcolm Lowry. Among a number of postwar alcoholics, he was the one whose literary work was most strongly affected by addiction; his most admired works move in and out of harrowing personal tragedy. To read *Under the Volcano* (1947) is to become closely involved with the Consul's losing battle with drink as well as to experience vividly the Mexican scene.

A *Malcolm Lowry*

In *Ultramarine* (1933), the narrative of a long voyage as sailor aboard the merchant ship *Oedipus Tyrannus*, Lowry had begun using the extended interior monologue, in which his youthful protagonist Dana Hilliot "moves in drunken fantasies from his mother to a Singapore brothel to a series of Latin cognates for God to a remembered headmaster to the words of a song about the Crucifixion." This, says Richard Costa, "is quite likely the first extended stream-of-consciousness by Lowry on the Joyce-Aiken model."9 Aiken is of course Conrad Aiken, with whom Lowry had a long and professionally profitable friendship. After coming to Canada in 1939, Lowry also became acquainted with a number of Canadian literary figures, including the poet-novelist Earle Birney, then at Vancouver, where Lowry lived in a beach shack (at Dollarton) which burned in 1945.

Under the Volcano, Lowry's one undoubted masterpiece, is simultaneously simple and complex. It is tragic in the classical sense that the ruin it describes is that of a fine-minded if not politically "great" man. Into the Consul's fantasies Lowry wove all kinds of symbols and muted references; his uses of, and relations to, various aspects of cabalism, alchemy, astrology, tarot, and other portions of his "magical universe" have been extensively explored in Tony Kilgallin's *Lowry*, published in 1973. Lowry's "one great statement," Costa believes, "carried the defects of its virtues" in that he "found it impossible to give his career a second act."10 *Ultramarine* and *Under the Volcano* are the only works published during Lowry's lifetime.

Lowry himself has become a cult figure, on the model of Ernest Hemingway or Dylan Thomas. W. H. New labels the 1960s "Lowry's decade" by contrast with the 1950s which were, in their realistic, comparatively settled outlook, "MacLennan's decade." Partly through the devotion of his widow and friends, partly through continuing interest in his previous work and ongoing legend, work left incomplete at his death has been edited and published. *Hear Us O Lord from Heaven Thy Dwelling Place* (1961), for which the Governor General's Award was given posthumously, is a collection of short stories differing widely in technique but all converging in their use of the voyage motif. A novella, *Lunar Caustic*, followed in 1963, and in 1970, *October Ferry to Gabriola*, a multilevelled exploration of the dispossession-

and-wandering theme again using mystical lore on somewhat the same scale as *Under the Volcano*.

B *Leonard Cohen*

The fiction of the poet-musician Leonard Cohen differs fundamentally from Lowry's in the roles assigned its chief characters. Whereas the Consul of *Under the Volcano* is a mature man struggling against himself to overcome a known weakness which he cannot control, seeking regeneration but unable to achieve it, Cohen's young Breavman is torn between love and cruelty in ways he cannot understand. Through Breavman (chief figure of *The Favorite Game*, 1963) the Jewish community of Montreal is described in variously pitched comment. Much of the action takes place in sundry bedrooms in Montreal or New York, but for all his searching Breavman finds himself able only to reject whatever love comes his way. He tells one of his women, half-seriously only, that there is no friendship apart from sexual practice: "A friendship between a man and a woman which is not based on sex is either hypocrisy or masochism": sex is "the vocabulary we speak in today . . . the only language left." When she protests that if that's so, then it's "a language which nobody understands. It's just become a babble," he replies: "Better than silence . . . ."[11] On the other hand, he is capable of emotions close to reverence, as in this brief scene in a brass foundry:

> Now a huge man wearing an asbestos apron and goggles took over. He guided the crucible over to the molds. With a lever device he tilted the stone pot and poured the molten brass into the lead-holes of the molds.
> Breavman gasped at the brightness of the liquid metal. It was the color gold should be. It was as beautiful as flesh. It was the color of gold he thought of when he read the word in prayers or poems. It was yellow, alive and screaming. It poured out in an arch with smoke and white sparks. He watched the man move up and down the rows, dispensing this glory. He looked a monolithic idol. No, he was a true priest.[12]

In *Beautiful Losers* (1966) a sexually agonized narrator turns to metaphysics for a way out of his troubles, seeking a spiritual communion with Catherine Tekakwitha, a seventeenth-century Iroquois saint. Opinion on this novel varies sharply. D. G. Jones sees it as "extending the insights of Lampman and Grove" (who saw, early, the threat of technocracy) and as pointing out that the "garrison mentality"—in itself an extension of colonial attitudes—

. . . persists in the highly aggressive but essentially very exclusive spirit informing much of our modern world . . . our comfort, our leisure, the means and the desire for sensual pleasure. It wars upon death; yet only complicates dying. It would make the world a new Eden; yet more often pollutes and destroys it.[13]

By contrast, Donald Cameron describes it in these terms:

Romping through sanctity, mysticism, free-form eroticism, politics and technology, the book concludes with the metamorphosis of the hero, now a stinking old man, into a Ray Charles movie projected on the sky. Breavman, O Breavman, how solid you seem now![14]

C   *Juan Butler, Timothy Findley, Dave Godfrey and Others*

No such ambiguities as Cohen's are permitted to clog the fiction of Juan Butler, who, as W.H. New suggests,

. . . creates shocking scenes not to titillate or reform, nor even to educate the middle class; rather, in presenting to his age a compact glimpse of what it has become, he is probing the tangible relationships between social structure and psychological motivation and offering a coherent, if often repellent, explanation of human behavior.[15]

The Garbageman (1972) affords us such a "compact glimpse" as the mood of the narrator, after a career including rape and murder, is summed up in what he says about his psychiatrist. Anything "the shrink" himself says is "of no importance anyways," since

Only his eyes matter. They're dirty and deceitful and are always following me around. They never leave me alone. I can feel them boring into my back right now this very minute. Like two laser beams cutting through concrete.

One day I'm going to tear them out of his head during one of those stupid sessions with him. Laugh at him. Leave him in a state of extreme shock with two unseeing jelly-like eyeballs bouncing against his cheeks, joined to bloody eye-sockets by thin, fibrish nerves. Let him feel what it's like to be treated like a guinea pig. To be mutilated like a corpse. To be ridiculed like a circus freak. To be considered a piece of garbage.

One day.[16]

And yet, horrendous as all this may sound, its effect is blunted by overwriting; it seems a revenger's tragedy evaporating into bombast. Butler's first novel, *Cabbagetown Diary: a Documentary* (1970), presents a diarist, Michael, who after one brush with the law does not reform but becomes a very careful manipulator of others. Another "autobiographical" crime-novel, *In the Belly of the Whale* (1974) by Don Bailey (the author began writing after a five-year prison term) is a crime-and-prison narrative of Joe Cross, who is left, at the end, on parole.

Timothy Findley, an actor-playwright, employs the novel to explore the theme of violence as the result of frustrated expectations: perfection is impossible, even though social tradition insists relentlessly that it *is* possible and must be sought for. *The Last of the Crazy People* (1967) is set in southern Ontario, *The Butterfly Plague* (1969) in southern California, but both describe later-twentieth-century decadence. Murder (within the family), incest, psychological holocausts of all sorts occur as results of the categorical inability of mortals to be gods. Perhaps it is no accident that Findley did television scripts for the *Jalna* saga; his Winslows and Damarosches seem to have arrived at "the dead end of the Family Compact," as Findley puts it.[17]

The last of this grouping, Dave Godfrey, published—first in 1967—*Death Goes Better with Coca-Cola*, then a deluxe edition in 1973 with fake-parchment pages and three-color printing, combined with old catalogue line-cuts, Chinese ideographs (and little moral essays), and other mock-elegant embellishments. The story-line takes on multiple dimensions as well, with adventures in Canada, various parts of the United States, and West Africa strung together. Among the numerous characters encountered are hunters, fishermen, American protesters against the Vietnam war, and members of the counter-culture. *The New Ancestors* (1970), a Governor General's Award winner, takes place in an imaginary West African setting, "Lost Coast" (maps are supplied), during the 1960s. It bears more than a coincidental resemblance to Ghana. There are political intrigues of all sorts, including strong-arm American action. The situation is summed up, to a degree, in the thoughts and words of Father Skelly, a departing priest:

These people didn't want to be harangued with clichés about reactionism and colonial mentality. Why not announce something constructive? Why not bring down some of the troops that had nothing to do but shoot down university students and track Samuel Hastings through the whole country, bring them down here to Silla to build housing for the fishermen?

"The trouble with our period," he said aloud, "is that we've forgotten that there were other times than the present. We can't look backwards at all . . . . Why the country's full of Samuels, Kofi, you must know that by now. You can't build jails fast enough to keep up with them, because they are nothing but imitations of Kruman himself. They see just how he gathered in the wealth—by saying us and doing I—and they follow him, they imitate him, they are him."[18]

The internationally minded reader will be interested in comparing this version of politics in Third-World Africa with such other novels as Peter Abrahams' *A Wreath for Udomo* (1956) or Chinua Achebe's *A Man of the People* (1966). We learn from Godfrey, says Anthony Boxill,

. . . that the fact and distress of ancestry affect all the characters alike, that Burdener and Harding, European and African, are the new ancestors, and that their offspring are inevitably going to be confronted with their past as they themselves have been.[19]

Both Africa and the West Indies have been given close attention in Canadian foreign policy for quite some time. West Indian migrants have become Canadian writers and scholars; other Canadian writers such as Margaret Laurence, Audrey Thomas, and Dave Godfrey have lived in Africa and written about it. To the works of these may be added *Farquharson's Physique and What It Did to His Mind* (1971) by David Knight, portraying a potential murderer who under strain in Nigeria becomes one.

III   *Feminism*

Modern Canadian women writers have an uncommon tradition behind their work. The first Canadian novelist, it will be recalled, was a woman; and it is no mere academic accident that the poet-critic-novelist Margaret Atwood turns back to Susanna Moodie as a spiritual mother-figure. Brooke, Moodie, Duncan, Montgomery, McClung, de la Roche—all these were professional writers in their time, and there were others. Any present-day reckoning would have to include, at a minimum, the names of Margaret Atwood, Marian Engel, Mavis Gallant, Margaret Laurence, Gwendolyn McEwen, Alice Munro, Sheila Watson, and Ethel Wilson—strong talents by any international standard, implying as well that the future of Canadian fiction is likely to be considerably more bisexual than in the past. Among these, thus far, Laurence is the leading figure. Beginning to write and publish at about the same time as these women, but cut off by an early death was Patricia Blondal, whose two posthumous novels predicted some of the more prominent attitudes later feminist writing was to reflect. The first, *A Candle to Light the Sun* (1960), describes life in a prairie town; the second, better-known *From Heaven With a Shout* (1963), takes a young widow from London to Vancouver to marry a wealthy Canadian who has advertised for a wife. Life among the western Canadian plutocracy is not, she finds, what she would have chosen.

A *Mavis Gallant and Others*

Both Margaret Laurence and Mavis Gallant are writers on the international scale, Laurence having begun her work in Africa and Gallant writing and publishing in Europe and the United States as well as Canada. Of Gallant, Edmund Wilson comments:

She is more international than Canadian in [her] later more elaborate stories [*My Heart Is Broken*, 1964] as in her novel *Green Water, Green Sky* [1959], adventuring about Europe, she gets away from the Canadian bleakness and her work displays a color and wit rather rare among native writers. She is excellent at evoking, by dialogue and detail, a variety of milieux, and the stories about Canada gain from their contrast with those that take place in the other parts of the world she has inhabited.[20]

A recent novel, *A Fairly Good Time* (1970), shows well this international orientation as well as the author's concern with feminine nature. It is a clever, humorous account of love and loneliness, exposing the pitfalls of lack of understanding and giving too much of oneself in a world unable to accept such giving. Shirley Perrigny, a Canadian woman with a strong feeling of responsibility toward anyone who needs help, is living in Paris during the 1960s after the tragic death of her first husband. A second marriage to Philippe Perrigny ends in divorce, Philippe being quite unable to understand Shirley's disorganized and impulsive but attractively witty and independent way of life. She appears doomed to destroy personal relationships with over-concern.

By contrast with such skillful technique, feminism defiantly on
the warpath is evident in more that one novel of the 1960s and 70s,
and its excited rhetoric may too easily run to extremes among
Canadian women authors as with those elsewhere. This is readily
shown by an example, taken from a novel published in 1970, the
same year as *A Fairly Good Time*. Here the heroine is describing
marriage as she views it from having observed her parents'
experience; and within a half-page the following words and
phrases (given in sequence) occur: *mess—bondage—suffering—
repetition—vindictively silent—bitter reproaches and outbursts—
rage—frustration—organized warfare—hostages—battle lines*. It
may well be that some marriages are all this, or even more, but is
the novelist's most effective approach a fire raid on the thesaurus?
In short fiction, Jane Rule's "Theme for Diverse Instruments" is
perhaps less a story than a semi-portrait/semi-diagram of a
composite woman whose trials and tribulations cohere into a
feminist manifesto, quite ably written.[21]

B   *Margaret Atwood, Marian Engel, Audrey Thomas*

Margaret Atwood in her fiction as well as in her poetic *Journals
of Susanna Moodie* (1970) and her critical volume *Survival* (1972)
develops emphatic ideas on the treatment and mistreatment of
women. Two novels, *The Edible Woman* (1969) and *Surfacing*,
(1973), offer both the panoramic and the individual points of view
on women's problems. The first, as suggested by the title, sees
women as social victims, bored with their jobs, involved in
quandaries over sex, and subject as a result to personality clashes.
The composite picture is one of confusion among the young, those
doing postgraduate study as well as those already finished with
college and working at jobs they despise. *Surfacing* takes the
narrator (not given a name) back to her girlhood background, the
wilderness of the Quebec lake country. Struggling to survive
emotionally and physically, she suffers a violent trauma after
finding the body of her lost father at the bottom of a lake. The
psychological symbolism in both setting and action is laced with
anti-technology and anti-Americanism (which tend to merge into
the same demon). An extended analysis of the novel by Roberta
Rubinstein reveals the anthropological complexity of the
narrator's fictional rebirth, involving "even further symbolic
regression into the collective unconscious."

Each act is saturated with mythic and metaphorical significance. After the others leave, she returns to the cabin and to her mother's garden. There she cries for the first time, releasing the emotion so long frozen inside her as she mourns her parents and her own past self. (The image of her in her mother's garden echoes the archetypal motif of the mother as a vegetation deity and nurturing figure.) Then she burns the nine years of her dead life encapsulated by marriage: her art briefcase, her wedding ring, the artifacts that must be "translated" (that is, assimilated) through the purification of fire. Nine, of course, suggests the human gestation period that she never completed, either literally with her own child, or psychologically with her self. Finally, she strips completely and cleanses herself by immersion once more in the lake.

After this mythic enactment of rebirth, the narrator finds taboos and directives everywhere; she exists in a state of primitive consciousness in which each object in the outer world is invested with sacred and personal significance. Everything remotely associated with human civilization is forbidden, even food and shelter. She eats roots and builds an animal-like lair. . . .[22]

Some readers might wonder whether so much metaphorical intricacy is altogether appropriate in a writer who sees social damnation in overelaborations of machinery: must the solution necessarily recapitulate the whole predicament? Does the comic treatment of much the same material in her third novel (*Lady Oracle*, 1976) suggest, possibly, a recognition of this?

At least in *Lady Oracle* the heroine Joan Foster *is* comic, though with a broad pathetic fringe to her life. What does this overstuffed ugly Canada gosling who grows up to be a writer of Costume Gothic fiction want from marriage, from life itself? She doesn't quite know, even after she has tricked herself into thinking she has killed the past and started over, in Italy of all places.

If you let one worm out of a can of worms, all the other worms will follow. Aunt Lou used to say that; she had many useful maxims, some traditional, some invented by her. For instance, I've heard "The tongue is the enemy of the neck" elsewhere, but never "There's more than one cat in any bag" or "Don't count on your rabbits before they're out of the hat." Aunt Lou believed in discretion, though only in important matters.[23]

Well, if there are anti-heroes why can't there be anti-heroines too? Why not, indeed? Joan's last word for us is "It did make a mess; but I don't think I'll ever be a very tidy person."[24]

A second pair of novels by Marian Engel—*The Honeyman*

Festival (1970) and *Bear* (1977)—shows us disturbed women both in city life and in the wilderness. In the first, Mina, now the mother of three children and eight months pregnant with her fourth, recalls her life in Paris where she had known a Hollywood producer (Honeyman) and other men and for various reasons wonders whether life has turned out the way she wanted it to. *Bear*, the author's fifth novel to date, takes a woman named Lou to an island in northern Ontario where the only other inhabitant is a bear. Close association with wild animal life, she comes to feel— dangerous as it may be—is somehow purifying.

Still another retreat to an island occurs in Audrey Thomas's pair of short novels, *Munchmeyer* and *Prospero on the Island* (1971). Like Margaret Laurence, Thomas resided for a time in Africa (Ghana), the setting for *Mrs. Blood* (1970): a white woman fearing a miscarriage finds herself divided into two selves, "Mrs. Blood" her intense personal self and "Mrs. Thing" her outer "objective" self. All her mental processes become involved in this split. A "sense of division" analogous to this, says one commentator, "seems to be fundamental to Thomas's world." [25]

C   Ethel Wilson

Ethel Wilson, whose career began with the portrayal of an "unorthodox" woman in *Hetty Dorval* (1947), continued to explore feminine behavior in four novels and a book of short stories, the latter appearing in 1961. In *The Swamp Angel* (1954) Maggie Vardoe, tiring of her role of wife and mother in Vancouver, moves out and takes up employment in the wilderness. Elizabeth Waterston sees this novel as containing several versions of "the Canadian lady" which come together in Maggie Vardoe.

> Maggie's is a triumph of withdrawal rather than of commitment. She is presented in a book admirable in an artistic sense, elegant, sophisticated, and modern. In her, we have a modern version of the perilous flight of the Canadian lady—the "swamp angel." But where is the portrait of the Canadian woman as a young, free, passionate person? Still to come . . . perhaps from the new world of Women's Liberation—where angels may well fear to tread. [26]

The retreat to the wilderness, as *The Swamp Angel* shows us, is not entirely a late twentieth-century idea. And how ironic that the

Canadian wife and mother, both fictional and real, who for two centuries or more has wanted nothing so much as to get out of the wilderness, should be so often envisaged as fleeing back to it.

D   *Poet-Novelists: Gwendolyn McEwen, Patricia K. Page*

Gwendolyn McEwen's search for a modern solution takes her to the past, as we observed at the beginning of this chapter. In addition to *King of Egypt, King of Dreams* she has published *Julian the Magician* (1963), which seems to recapitulate Christ's life through Julian, who is poignantly aware of the parallelism. The stories in *Noman* (1972) make extensive use of myth, which is seen as the key to human adjustment in contemporary chaos.

Current interest in myth, which in Canada has long been fostered by Northrop Frye's attention to, and advocacy of, the work of Jung, may have had something to do with the republication of a novelette by Patricia K. Page, another poet-novelist, *The Sun and the Moon* (1944), to which has been added a number of short stories in a 1973 volume which has an introduction by Margaret Atwood. The title story's heroine, Kristin, possesses special powers because of her birth during a lunar eclipse; she may take over other people's souls, including that of her lover and at-length husband Carl Bridges, a painter, with predictably tragic consequences. (So, one may ask, there are edible males as well?) There is something of Kristin in the other stories, too. "Their language," says Margaret Atwood, "is, in general, more condensed, and their footwork more adroit, . . . but they share . . . both the bizarre perspective and the disconcerting insights characteristic of Page's work at its best."[27]

E   *Emily Carr: Autobiographic Fiction*

The writings of the artist Emily Carr, strictly speaking, are chiefly autobiography but their tone is at least semifictional and— not surprising in a major artist—the descriptions are finely wrought. Her chief volumes of prose are *Klee Wyck* (1941), *The Book of Small* (1942), *The House of All Sorts*(1944), and *Growing Pains* (1946). "Because she knew almost nothing of the mechanics of writing," says Ira Dilworth, her friend and editor, in his introduction to *The House of All Sorts,*

. . . she was uninhibited by many of the restraints that formal instruction places upon the creative artist. Sentence and paragraph structure meant nothing to her; correctness in spelling and punctuation, if possible, even less. But she had a natural gift in the choice of words, a frank Anglo-Saxon daring in the use of metaphor, and an unerring sense of form that never left her. As she wrote she had the ability to live so completely in the experience she described that she conjured it up with vivid reality before the reader, or, more correctly perhaps, snatched him up and took him there with her.

Emily Carr herself had advice for writers well worth heeding, as for instance:

Be careful that you do not write or paint anything that is not your own, that you don't know in your own soul . . . if you make your own cake and *know the recipe and stir the thing with your own hand* it's *your* own cake. You can ice it or not as you like. Such lots of folks are licking the icing off the other fellow's cake.[28]

Other, more recent autobiography in totally fictional form takes quite a different tone from Emily Carr's acceptance of her world and the pleasure to be found in it. Ronald Sutherland's *Lark des Neiges* (1971—an extended treatment of a disturbed woman, somewhat a rarity among male writers) chronicles the unhappy life of Suzanne Laflamme, under the pressures of lower-class Montreal. She tells a sympathetic listener:

It's taken me a long time to realize a lot of things, Minnie. And it's a bloody pity it took me so long, because otherwise I might have been able to be myself a long time ago. I can see it now.
   The big trouble with me is that I've never really been able to be myself. Chienne de vie! Nobody would let me—my father, my mother, the whole damned world. My mind has always been tangled up. I wanted to do what I was supposed to do, but I was never sure what the hell it was I was supposed to do. Or at least I had a few pretty weird ideas. Calvaire! It's amazing how a whole pile of things can prevent a person simply from being herself. C'est pas un cadeau.[29]

By contrast with Suzanne's self-pity (one almost expects her to wind up by saying "I've never been able to be myself because I hadn't the slightest idea what I wanted to be"), Sharon Riis's short first novel, *The True Story of Ida Johnson* (1977), presents in folk idiom the oral autobiography (told for a fee of twenty dollars) of a waitress in a roadside hashery near "Longview," Alberta. Ida tries hard to rid herself of all "bullshit" illusions about virtually all of life, succeeding in talking as objectively about slitting the throats of her husband and children as she does about her Indian friend Lucy. As a counterweight to elaborately contrived symbolic agonistics by some other heroines in the Canadian landscape, the "clean clean perfect clean slice" of Ida's butcher knife may have something to recommend it. Fortunately, however, there are other choices; not quite every maladjusted woman is a compulsive Clytemnestra.

F *Alice Munro and Others*

Novels and story collections chronicling the transit through girlhood are by now as common in Canadian fiction as the traditional male *Bildungsroman*. Some of the more recent ones include works by Elizabeth Brewster, Sylvia Fraser, and Alice Munro, all writing in the 1970s. Brewster's *The Sisters* (1974) is set in small towns in New Brunswick during the 1930s and through the war years of the 40s; it takes the narrator, Jane, from the age of nine to twenty-three and embraces as well the parallel lives of her sisters Lottie and Vickie. Fraser's *Pandora* (1972) likewise takes place during the period of World War II hysteria and misery, in "Mill City" (i.e., Hamilton, Ontario). It brings Pandora Gothic to the age of eight in a densely packed record of experience, suggesting that if her name is symbolic (as it seems obviously intended to be), Pandora does not need to open any box of evils— it is already wide open for her when she comes into the world. Through her sharp childhood vision the adult world, as well, is revealed. Like Mary Peate's *Girl in a Red River Coat* (1970—cited in Chapter 3 as a latter-day counterweight to *Anne of Green Gables*), *Pandora* is grimly realistic. Fraser's *The Candy Factory* (1975) is both a commercial and a sexual extravaganza.

Jane Rule, in *Against the Season* (1971), approaches deviant sexuality with both dignity and compassion. In one comment on the everlasting dilemma of women, this exchange takes place:

"So many people—women—never do find anything they like to do. Or anyway they don't make a career of it. Miss Setworth should have been an English teacher. But it's easier for us, in our generation, I guess."
"A woman should marry," Dina said.

"Really? All women?" Harriet asked, surprised.

"Any woman."

"Easier said than done," Harriet answered, immediately embarrassed by what she had said.[30]

The complex of personal relationships which the novel explores includes—in addition to lesbianism—middle-aged courtship, anticipation of death by the aged, childbirth, difficulties long past but revealed through a diary, and at one point the love-poetry of Yeats. Jane Rule has also published *The Desert of the Heart* (1964) and *This Is Not For You* (1970).

Alice Munro's *Lives of Girls and Women* (1971) and *Something I've Been Meaning to Tell You* (1974) are both story collections affording a wide spectrum of women characters, young and old, as is a similar collection by Joyce Marshall, *A Private Place* (1975). *Lives of Girls and Women* is set in a small town where "Stories of the past could go round like this, round and round and down to death; I expected it."[31] Social realism is applied unsparingly to the record of a girl's growth toward full womanhood; the mother, aunts, and girlhood friends appear among various small crises and revelations. There are songs, sights, customs, and sayings, with two full chapters on religion ("Age of Faith" and "Baptizing"), and two other "initiation" chapters ("Changes and Ceremonies" and the title story). *Something I've Been Meaning to Tell You* offers several mother stories, dealing quite differently with each woman. Settings vary between town and farm, and there is careful attention to the buffetings of love suffered by older people as well as adolescents. In recently published interviews, Munro is refreshingly iconoclastic about a great deal of the critical rhetoric on technique—symbolism, for instance.

G   Margaret Laurence

Margaret Laurence is less experimental than some of her younger colleagues, who very much admire her and take strength from her achievements as well as from the substantial amount she has written (and spoken, in interviews) on the craft of fiction and the novelist's pleasures and perils. She too has published a story-cycle on growth, *A Bird in the House* (1970), in which young Vanessa of the semi-prairie town "Manawaka" (Manitoba; Neepawa, northwest of Winnipeg, is where Laurence was born and reared) experiences family crises, friendships, and opposition (most notably between Vanessa and her stern Scots grandfather Connor). The episodes do not occur in a connected sequence but the net effect is closer to a novel than to the usual assemblage of stories, and they form part of a Manawaka group which includes *The Stone Angel* (1964), *A Jest of God* (1966), *The Fire-Dwellers* (1969), and *The Diviners* (1974). If we wished to view the whole series as a panorama of female experience all the way to old age, we would need to place *A Bird in the House* first and *The Stone Angel* last—an order which in a sense is technically climactic as well.

In *A Jest of God*, then, we encounter a spinster schoolteacher, Rachel Cameron, encapsulated in a *froufrou* apartment with her mother, longing in her mid-thirties for sexual fulfillment and motherhood of her own. At length she manages a summer-long affair with a lover she cannot understand, nor he her, and at the end of the novel she takes her mother (who has become in effect her child: "I am the mother now," she tells herself) to Vancouver, where she has another job.

Stacy MacAindra, of *The Fire-Dwellers*, is another Manawaka girl now in Vancouver—married and an actual mother as Rachel longed to be, but nevertheless with problems: her marriage teeters and nearly collapses. Stacy's story is told with humor and sensitive interpretation both of people (children included) and the situations that develop between them.

The Diviners brings us to middle age, in which the central character, Morag Gunn, is a well-known Canadian novelist who at age 47 reviews her life. Her marriage with Brooke Shelton, an academic, is falling apart; and having purchased a small farm in Ontario where she can have solitude for writing, she seeks new friendships as well as assurance in her recollections. Recalling her stepfather Christie Logan, a garbageman, and watching a neighbor Royland, a water diviner, she wonders about her own powers of divination as a writer. In Jules Tonnerre, a Métis, she begins to sense a bond springing from a mutual sense of dispossession and hostility to upper-class pretension.

Laurence began her career with a series of books on Somaliland and Ghana, where she and her engineer husband spent the years 1950–57. Her publications emerging from this experience were partly documentary, partly fictional—not just apprentice-work, but stories and descriptions prophetic of a Canadian interest in

African themes that was to become more evident some years later. She had developed, as Clara Thomas puts it, "an empathy for Africa and its people":

. . . the deepest springs of her compassion are for them and the surest parts of her skill are at their service. She knows Africans in their own settings and she sketches background, in all its sensual detail, with absolute authority, not only with its sights and sounds, but with the authentic realities of smell and taste added for their maximum effect, an all-dimensional otherworld for the reader's reception.[32]

When Laurence returned to Canada, her first Canadian novel, *The Stone Angel*, received enthusiastic reception. Its author was, as Harrison tells us, "probably the nearest of the younger writers to the prairie realists in spirit and in method, which may help to explain why *The Stone Angel* is the more thoroughly realized fiction of the period so far."[33]

Hagar Shipley, the protagonist of *The Stone Angel*, has a biblical name not lightly bestowed. One product of Laurence's upbringing in a Calvinist community was a thorough knowledge of the Bible, which surfaces repeatedly in her work. Hagar, living now the last few weeks of a very long life, is presented through her own consciousness "rampant with memory," self-probing, alternating between past and present, resisting as best she can the decay and death that advanced age inevitably brings, despising her condition and the surroundings in which she must play out her last act. She is intended as an ambiguous character, one for whom the reader must feel both admiration and hostility, for she is more often than not, as her own son concedes, "a holy terror." She comes to know this herself:

Pride was my wilderness, and the demon that led me there was fear. I was alone, never anything else, and never free, for I carried my chains with me, and they spread out from me and shackled all I touched. Oh, my two, my dead. Dead by your own hands, or by mine? Nothing can take away those years.[34]

As a portrait of old age, severe but truthful, *The Stone Angel* bears comparison with other treatments of the same subject, perhaps most notably Patrick White's *The Eye of the Storm* (1973).

Margaret Laurence believes that in fiction which works as it should—certainly in those parts of her own fiction which have worked best for the reader—the character is palpably separate from the writer, not a mere mask. In establishing the narrative voice, the character must choose parts of the past which "have to be revealed in order for the present to be realized and the future to happen."[35] Thus, time *and* voice are the life-stuff of fiction. The Manawaka novels and stories are a massive composite testimonial to these creative principles.

Finally, two passages—both from recent works—serve to emphasize the growing distance between older views taken of elders by the young and newer ones. In the first, from Ebbitt Cutter's brief but ingratiatingly composed "Laurentian Idyll," *The Last Noble Savage* (1967), a woman gives her semifictional girlhood recollections of an Indian house-servant, Madame Dey, who was adequate to all emergencies, great or small. Summing up,

Not only did she survive in the 20th century by her ancient Indian skills and values, but she shamed that world, showing up the hollowness of many of its most dearly-held pretensions about itself.

The second, from Beth Harvor's *Women and Children* (1973), presents two daughters' interpretation of their mother:

As for her daily forays downtown, they decided that it was not so much what she was escaping *from* (they, after all, took care of that), as what she was escaping *to*; it was apparent to them that her trips downtown gave her back herself. They lamented that none of the other kids had mothers like *her*, other kids they knew didn't even want to *talk* about their mothers, but Chrissie and Anne talked about Katie almost continuously; in their minds she was oppressor, specimen, curiosity, star. And they imagined her, their morning's oppressor and star, downtown, buoyed up by the glances of the men, preening herself in her mind. They knew that finally, at morning's end, her arms loaded with bounty from the A U P (where the cashier was always so cheerful and kind), she would return home, rehabilitated.[36]

IV *Academic Life*

During the late 1960s the counter-culture movements in and around universities virtually everywhere stood out in so strong a light of publicity that it should be no surprise to find academic life one of the prominent themes of recent Canadian fiction. It is true, as well, that quite a number of recent Canadian novelists are themselves academics, although they do not write voluminously about student life, leaving that task (wisely enough) to the more ambitious among their students. Fiction with Academia as its setting, in Canada or elsewhere, does not commonly reach great heights for reasons that are fairly self-evident: the crises of that relatively short period a person spends in college or university, while very real and sometimes agonizing, are usually not the most important in life. Several novels bearing on this topic are mentioned here, and further treatments are available in short stories.

Two titles, the second already discussed, may be recalled here as having in quite different fashions an academic context: Robertson Davies's *Leaven of Malice* (1954) and Morley Callaghan's *A Fine and Private Place* (1975). *Leaven of Malice* (winner of the Leacock Medal for Humour in the year of its publication) uses a practical joke—the publication of a false notice of engagement between a university instructor and a professor's daughter—as the "leaven of malice and wickedness" which Scripture urges us to put away. The academic satire involves, among other things, some ludicrous comment on a new branch of English study known as "Amcan"—"a new field in literary study, particularly the Can half."

A few years later, appropriately enough for the times, Jack Ludwig's *Confusions* (1963) is explained by its author as "a grappling hook." What it grapples with is American academic life, especially in California, in a scenario with directional signals like "The White-Shoe Man's Burden," "Thoreau in California," "Sisyphus: Labor to Be Beautiful!" and "Out in Left Field, Lonely." The confused academic scene apparently fits Ludwig's fictional pattern as described by a fellow-novelist, Dave Godfrey, commenting on a later work, *Above Ground* (1968):

> What Ludwig has done is to violently wrench the novel form to fit modern society, stealing all the richness and potential of short fiction and making a chronicle out of an anthology, a long myth out of selected metamorphoses, an epic voyage out of his own lusthungerings and memoryfarings and lifethrustings.[37]

Less comprehensively, George Bowering's *Mirror on the Floor* (1967) describes graduate student Bob Small's summertime affair with Andrea, ending with complications in the course of which, as the newspaper headline expressed it, BEATNIK GIRL SLAYS MOTHER. John Peter's *Shake Hand with Winter* (also 1967) is set in a college in western Canada. Norman Levine's university experience at McGill enters into his stories frequently, along with other references to school. In *From a Seaside Town* (1970), a writer, Joseph Banks, reviews early events of his life in Ottawa and Montreal, including McGill; and in "A Small Piece of Blue" (from *I Don't Want To Know Anyone Too Well*, 1971) an alcoholic doctor-poet named Crepeau, at a northern Ontario mine, explains to a visiting student from McGill his views of what a university education does for, and to, the individual:

> The conversation jumped from the campus, to Montreal, to sport, to the different places we had seen. "Look at yourself," he suddenly interrupted, "You talk. You can talk like I can. We both can make talk. Talk on anything. They have seen to that. But what good does it do you, or anybody else? They've sandpapered all your rough edges, your instincts, your intuitions, then turned you out with a false smartness like a car on the assembly line. You happen to be the 1950 model. I was the 1933. The funny thing is we like it."[38]

Couched in the student vernacular of the uncertain later 1960s, *Five Legs* (1969) by Graeme Gibson divides into two sections headed "Lucan" and "Felix," a teacher and a student, respectively, at the University of Western Ontario. The first portion takes us into Lucan's mind during a wintry drive to the funeral of a student killed by a hit-and-run driver. Quarrels, gossip, and attempts at sustained conversation are interspersed with interior monologue. "Felix" (the dead student's roommate) is handled similarly, with contrasts between calm, ceremonial politeness and the violent disorder within the mind. Both *Five Legs* and *Communion* (1971), says Norah Story, contain fire and animal symbolism which suggests ". . . a parallel between modern society headed towards self-destruction and the unfulfilled man who is unable to reconcile his spiritual aspirations with the repressive canons of the modern 'elect.'"[39]

In lighter vein, Tony Aspler's *The Streets of Askelon* (1972) evokes contemporary Montreal through the somewhat bloodshot eyes of Bart Shea, an Irish poet on lecture tour. Bart's precipitous troubles with wine and women, soon after his arrival, lead local authorities to cancel his song, scheduled for McGill University. This, not unnaturally, brings on a row. Befriended by a young woman journalist, Bart does not improve his habits. The invocation on page 1, "Samuel Butler you should be living at this hour," sets the satiric tone.

Academics themselves inhabit several other novels. In Marian
Engel's first novel, *No Clouds of Glory!* (1968), Dr. Sarah Porlock
finds herself dissatisfied with the Canadian literature in which she
has specialized and concludes that the academic mode of thinking
has rendered her cold—a problem that enters again into *The
Honeyman Festival* (1970). Matt Cohen's *Korsoniloff* (1969) describes the breakdown, into schizophrenia, of a philosophy professor. Speaking of the novel in an interview with Graeme Gibson,
Cohen reveals some of the motivations for writing it:

> *Gibson:* He [Korsoniloff] is an intellectual; he is almost a mockery of an
> intellectual in many ways, in a kind of humorous way, but it's a very
> destructive way. I mean to say is the university a measure of
> Korsoniloff's more desperate straits?
> *Cohen:* Yes. The university demands a consistent self-destruction and
> abstraction that's fairly unique, a very high level compared to what
> most other life courses demand.
> *Gibson:* The whole educational system then is the process of adapting
> to forms, eh? Is that what happens to Korsoniloff?
> *Cohen:* Yes, because you have to take as real what is totally unreal, and
> in order to do that you have to destroy what is real in yourself.[40]

Hugh Hood's *The Swing in the Garden* (1976) presents the
narrator's father as a professor of philosophy with too-liberal
economic and political ideas who in the 1930s resigns his post in
protest, "declaring that he could no longer profess philosophy in
an institution that served reactionary, arch-conservative interests."[41] Academic life and educational ideas, accordingly, come in
for rather frequent mention in this novel. Finally, in Brian Moore's
The Great Victorian Collection (1975) a young history professor
from McGill, Anthony Maloney, goes to California for a seminar
at Berkeley. During a visit to Carmel, he "dreams" a collection of
Victorian antiques which upon awakening he finds is real: his
dream-mind has in some way been able to materialize

> . . . Victorian silver tea sets, bridal breakfast services, ornamental urns,
> statuary, cheval glasses, tallboys, ottomans, poufs, corner cupboards,
> gaming tables, stoves, kitchen utensils, fireguards and firedogs . . . the
> parlor of a famous Victorian brothel and a room containing the furnish-
> ings of a Victorian music hall.[42]

Although it might at first seem that dreaming such treasures into
reality would bring the dreamer fame and fortune, that is not

quite the result. If Maloney's case is typical, such parapsychological manifestations are not to be longed for or taken lightly if achieved. Much of the story is tangential only to Academia, but there are some scenes laid in its bowers. More on the subject is to be found in contemporary short stories. Also in Moore's *Fergus* (1970) the element of fantasy, not surprising in any Irish writer, appears again in a California setting, where a novelist-filmwriter wakes up one morning to find his long-dead Irish parents present, and understandably, influencing his life. Finally, we note in these particular novels of Moore's—in contrast to his earlier work—a dependence on the fantastic which points us toward the next broad area of subject-matter.

V *Fantasy and Parable*

Fantasy, in our time, has established, or reestablished, itself in all literary modes, fiction not the least among them. So large a topic as this can be explored here only briefly, with the purpose of suggesting its pervasiveness. In fact, we have already encountered it in writers such as Lowry, Moore, and Atwood. Among the following group we shall find two exceptionally gifted fabulists, Sheila Watson and Robertson Davies, whose work is highlighted by that of others. Looking for origins of the topic, we think of myth and folklore, especially such as that springing from the continuing presence of aboriginal peoples as well as the large accretions of folklore through immigration. The strong influence of Jungian mythicism upon Canadian literature is proverbial. Psychological and sociological disturbances in the contemporary world are likewise productive of fantasy, though at the same time we have to remember that the poetic, the playful, are—fortunately—human constants. Finally, the methods of film and television have done a great deal to render fantasy and the Aesopian, parabolical method both widely prevalent and acceptable.

Sheila Watson's *The Double Hook*, up to now her only book-length work of fiction, was published in 1959 as if ushering in, intuitively, the turbulent 1960s. To read and re-read this short work is, first of all, to feel the impact of a most remarkable style. Its hard-hammered prose—"tight as rawhide"—is a superb narrative vehicle and at the same time shares its folk-speech rhythms with poetry and drama. Few of the words are of more than two syllables, and the beat is strongly monosyllabic throughout; accordingly, the sentences are short—somewhat biblically so. The story is as symbolic and archetypal as the most ardent disciple of Northrop Frye would wish, but it is very careful not to advertise itself as such. (An incisive interpretation of the mystical roles of two women in the book—the mother both as Nature and Woman, and Greta as Ice-goddess—appears in Margaret Atwood's *Survival*.) There is reward, too, for the eye as for the ear: the austere mountain landscape and the figures in it are evoked with quick sentences and phrases like brush strokes. John Grube's introduction to the NCL edition (1966) observes that the technique closely resembles the methods of film:

The cry of the coyote, the parched ground, James riding home over the hills, all would evoke a direct and unconscious response in the film viewer. The powerful dramatic element would also come to the fore, the snatches of dialogue alternative with moments when the camera eye lingered on significant detail.[43]

The theme of *The Double Hook*, supported with abundant fishing imagery, is that "when you fish for the glory you catch the darkness too."[44] Catching the darkness is never far below the laconic speech in which the characters converse. For example,

Lenchen will suffer like the rest of us, the Widow said. She's done wrong.
Right and wrong don't make much difference, Ara said. We don't choose what we will suffer. We can't even see how suffering will come.
She tossed the shirt onto the couch under the windows.
I never see baby-clothes, she said, that I don't think how a child puts on suffering with them.[45]

We feel the intermittent tug at the end of the line rather than beholding any moral "exposed in the white light like a hawk pulled out and pinned up on a barn door for all to see" (p. 59), and all the way through we are held close to the action. Some of the events are commonplace-seeming but exceptionally rendered (the Widow's boy wrestling with a kinky roll of wire, and at the same time with his own ungovernable thoughts; James withdrawing his money from the bank); others are highly spectacular (Greta's death by fire). Whatever the force of particulars may be, the whole performance is deliberately muted, very carefully modulated. Sometimes that talk is apparently only workaday chat; at other times, always retaining its lean idiom, it probes into ultimates, as in this passage where William and Ara, discussing human behavior, compare men with horses: horses may knock down fences and kick their way out of corrals only to come "wandering back to the barn and the hay."

Some, he said, are pure outlaw. But there's the torment of loneliness and the will of snow and heat they can't escape, and the likelihood that some stranger will put a rope on them at last.

Or perhaps even the man that branded them, Ara said. There are some men I suppose who follow, their ropes coiled and waiting. Sometimes I think of God like that, she said. The glory of his face shaded by his hat. Not coaxing with pans of oats, but coming after you with a whip until you stand and face him in the end.

I don't know about God, William said. Your god sounds only a step from the Indian's Coyote. Though that one would jump on a man when his back was turned. I've never seen God, he said, but if I did I don't think I'd be very much surprised.

I don't suppose you would, Ara said. Then she picked up the dishes and put them in the pan.[46]

If in all of modern Canadian fiction there is one diamond-hard yet beautifully faceted gem, surely this short novel must be it.

Other efforts at dealing with human conduct through apparently simple, artless fictional technique have had far less impact than *The Double Hook*. Matt Cohen's *Too Bad Galahad* (1972) is one such; another is Gladys Hindmarsh's *The Peter Stories* (1976) in which the familiar nursery-rhyme "Peter Peter, pumpkin eater" is given children's-book format and linguistic structure but adult content. These tend to bounce too easily off the reader's mind, as *The Double Hook* does not.

Douglas Le Pan, in *The Deserter* (1964)—"a formal invention designed to explore a theme,"[47] D. G. Jones calls it—evokes in his hero, Rusty, the double image of a man who recalls perfection (in Althea, loved and lost) and rejects the world of imperfect, base, disorderly experience (represented in another girl, Anne). Avoiding pursuit by both military authorities and the police (he has become associated with an underworld figure, Steve, who is finally murdered by his gang), Rusty has a dream of another underworld, a drowned realm on the seabed, and hears voices. Brought to rock-bottom, so to speak, his memories and residual courage are enough—only barely so—to enable him to commence rebuilding his life. Submission to the "devouring element" in Conradian terms—to the irrational in a sense—is the only rational course. A novel by Robert Hunter, *Erebus* (1968), set in Winnipeg, uses somewhat similar contrasting experiences of the disoriented hero in the Island (serenity, sanity, love) and the Slaughterhouse. Nigel Foxell's *Carnival*, published the same year, constructs an imaginary German place called Glommenheim, which apparently is romantic enough to inspire such outbursts as this (Walter is speaking of Lulu):

She was alcohol: set a match to her and she would be fire. My single sip of her was a conflagration in the arteries, a Vesuvius to erupt and gush in scoriac torrents, and I was ready to wash half the principality of Glommenheim into cinders.[48]

Still another imaginative Nowhere is Muddiman Castle of James Burke's *The Firefly Hunt* (1969), inherited from an eccentric uncle by Timothy Badger. Timothy's enjoyments of Muddiman Castle (somewhere in Canada, vaguely suggestive of Mervyn Peak's *Ghormengast*) are shared by his former landlady, an attractive woman of thirty-eight, and by a wino friend, Joe Bezoar, who

. . . looked quite neat, pressed, tidy, but a faint air of ancient, rancid human grease seeped from him. I thought he looked better on the carwash line in rough, ragged, frankly dirty work-clothes. Now he looked like the majority stockholder in a small egg mending factory on the day before bankruptcy.[49]

This Arcadian-bacchanalian existence is interrupted by a theft-and-flight episode involving attempted escape in a balloon, after which Timothy returns to the castle and a life of retirement from the World Out There.

Such excursions into humorous, semisatirical fantasy are continued in the early 1970s in works by Martin Myers (*The Assignment*, 1971) and George McWhirter (*Bodyworks*, 1974). *The Assignment* uses film terminology and to a degree film technique to present a disjointed series of episodes and encounters centering more or less in Speigel the Junk Man with an empty pushcart. There is straight narrative, dialogue, and other methods suggested by such chapter titles as "Montage," "Sneak Preview," "Off-Camera Voice," and "Out Takes." *Bodyworks* divides into three sections—"Aquatics," "Sarneatics and Close Alliances," and "The Asbestos Matrix"—masks for "trips" in varying degrees of fantasy.

Political fantasy, on the other hand, remains comparatively realistic in its supporting detail. In Richard Rohmer's *Ultimatum* (1973) the United States, desperate for oil resources, finally takes over Canada. Palma Harcourt's *Climate for Conspiracy* (1974) explains in an author's note that "for the purposes of this work of fiction it is assumed that Canada has left the Commonwealth and become a Republic, with a President as Head of State." *The Crazy House* (1975) by Anthony Brennan, however, is less specific. The scene is a fictitious northern country, a police state with two rival generals, Kurtal and Rankin. Part of the plot involves an art theft by the central figure Ned and his eccentric Uncle Dan. Love interest is supplied by Ned's mistress Carol, on the run from Kurtal's secret police. None of these novels seems to offer a great deal more than passable entertainment.

The work of Robertson Davies divides rather sharply between an earlier group of comico-satirical novels, the "Salterton" trilogy (discussed in Chapter 5) and later works in which the issues are more painful and the society represented, though more cosmopolitan, is far less stable and sure of itself than the remote small-city world of Salterton, Ontario. *Fifth Business* (1970) does, however, begin in another Ontario town, Deptford, in 1908. It introduces three boys, "Boy" Staunton, Paul Dempster, and Dunstan Ramsay, following the latter from boyhood to old age. The plot includes a vivid World War I scene in the battle of Passchendaele, skips lightly over Ramsay's service as master at a boys' school (1924–1969), but deals more extensively with three miracles in the life of Paul's mother, experiences which prompt him to do research on saints. While "Boy" Staunton becomes a captain of industry, Paul Dempster joins a circus and eventually returns as a notable magician, Magnus Eisengrim; through him, Ramsay meets his Devil and learns about Fifth Business.

The Manticore (1972) presents as its central character "Boy" Staunton's son David, a prominent Toronto lawyer who becomes mentally disturbed at the death of his father and seeks psychiatric help from a woman, Dr. Johanna von Haller. Much of his previous life is revealed through the Jungian analysis he undergoes. Still carrying on his profession, he goes to Europe, where he meets another Fraulein Doktor Liselotte (Liesl) Naegeli, with whom he visits an Alpine cave and sees into the nature of his primitive ancestors, arguing about this with Liesl. After an unnerving exit from the cave, in total darkness, he is left shaken and, at the conclusion, still bewildered. Liesl, from this novel, and Dunstan Ramsay from *Fifth Business* both figure again in the story of Magnus Eisengrim, related by himself in *World of Wonders* (1975). This novel, along with the adventure it recounts, touches on myth, magic, film, theater, God and the Devil.

In their analysis of Davies's use of the trickster in his novels, the critics R. M. Brown and D. A. Bennett have a great deal to say about the pervasive presence of Jungian psychology and comment broadly on the relationship of Davies's fiction to that of his contemporaries:

The emergence of a shamanistic trickster as a culture hero in Canadian fiction tells us much about the way the Canadian artist views his society just now. A new emphasis on individual freedoms has displaced the importance traditionally given social stability. The ideal of selfless sacrifice seems less desirable than the goal of personal survival. The problem of Job is being, not solved, but responded to—with the example of Prometheus. The hero is no longer Adam-like, losing his innocence and falling into culture; rather he defies the powers that would restrain him, making his own raids on the forbidden mysteries of the divine.[50]

In its extensive use of the occult, Davies's trilogy provides a saga that is the most distinguished exemplar of its type in contemporary fiction.

VI *Searching for THE Canadian Novel*

When artists begin ridiculing one another and joking about their art, it argues that a certain degree of maturity has been reached. In the 1970s we can see this commencing to happen to Canadian fiction: as if in response to the comedian Johnny Wayne's jibe of 1968—"Support your fellow Canadians. We should buy lousy Canadian novels instead of importing lousy American novels"—some of the novelists, at least, soon began to be less than solemn about their craft and its products. Meanwhile, the poet John Robert Colombo had added (in 1967) his bit with a dozen three-line stanzas of a "Recipe for a Canadian Novel," specifying one Indian, one Mountie, one Eskimo, one Doukhobor, to which should be added "one smalltown whore," "two thousand miles of wheat" complete with farmer "impotent and bent" and his fair-haired daughter, "then a Laurentian mountain and a Montreal Jew." Other ingredients include "a young boy with a dying pet," "a mortgage unmet," "exotic and tangy place names" (Toronto, Saskatoon, Hudson Bay). There is further mention of maple syrup, maple leaves, "one Confederation poet complete with verse," all of which is to be garnished with a sauce of "paragraphs of bad prose that never seem to stop." When simmered (but not brought to a boil) and baked, this concoction "Serves twenty million all told—when cold."[51]

In 1971, *The Latchkey Kid* by June Bhatia used a novel within a novel to spin its plot: Hank Stuch, whose mother Olga is so busy with social welfare that her son is a town waif (in "Tollemarche," Alberta), grows up and becomes the pseudonymous author of a sensational (and successful) novel, published in New York, called *The Cheaper Sex.* Ignorant of its authorship, Olga takes it as a symbol of all the objectionable literature her Committee for the Preservation of Morals is striving to have banned. When the trap is sprung, Olga is understandably put down, and there are further complications. The year following, Robert Harlow's *Scann* and Harry J. Boyle's *The Great Canadian Novel* both devoted themselves to anatomizing fiction and writers of fiction. Amory Scann, a novelist, is observed from four points of view: as writer, editor, seducer, and reminiscer (about World War II). John Moss's review in *Fiddlehead* was sympathetic: Harlow "fuses" his four dimensions well, using language which "overwhelms with its sheer efficiency, with its lucidity and vigour, with its visceral impact."[51] Boyle, a well-known Canadian humorist (winner of the Leacock Medal in 1964 and 1976), creates a Toronto advertising man, Shane Donovan, age fifty, who finally sickens of the rat-race and of his own unequal battle against alcoholism. After a lurid fling in New York he retreats to Mexico, dries out, and writes a book, meanwhile thinking about other Canadian novelists, for the most part not very flatteringly: MacLennan (whom he once met in a washroom), Mowat, Callaghan ("dated"), Richler ("expatriate," etc.), and Buckler, "the only one he enjoyed"—"a truly contemporary Thoreau." Still, he was rather "haunted" by Mitchell's *Who Has Seen the Wind.* After his "mental meanderings" subside, he concludes: "He was a Canadian and that means he had been conceiving and feeling in foreign images while thumping for a realization of what he imagined to be his own."[53] After this he feels a little more sympathetic toward Callaghan et al., and a letter from a publisher friend accepting the book is practically an invitation to join the club.

Not to neglect the more youthful beginner, one of George Bowering's stories tells us "How Desling Met Frances & Started to Write a Novel":

> I think Desling is already writing a novel at the time, about a kid who rises to the heights as a baseball player and then throws it all away for some moral gesture. So he's already noting the rhythms of the talk around him. How do you like the dames in the class! (1947, dig?) Jesus, how come all the ugly dames are always in our class? Jesus, did you notice the one in the Girl Guide suit? Agghh. . . [54]

What, then, *has* the Canadian novel been? We have encountered most of what John Colombo sets out in his formula, if not always in quite the same close context. Achievements in Canadian fiction were sporadic until well into the twentieth century, but in the last twenty-five to thirty years both the novel and the short story have deepened their roots and gathered impressive total strength. Until lately, the novel has stayed close to its national subject-matter, being eloquent on the varying face of the land itself and attracted to historical themes. Now it is reaching toward international content, but at no time has it been a mere echo of British or American practice. It is adequately—perhaps more than adequately—subjected to competent criticism. Occasionally capable of humor but seldom of really mordant satire, it is serious about minorities but is not yet confronting the French-English problem on a very broad scale. It is open to numerous experimental techniques which find ready publication. In short, it is not only a strong senior partner in Commonwealth fiction but an expanding area of composite World English.

Notes and References

N.B.-Special abbreviations are used throughout these notes for items cited with some frequency (for full data see the Bibliography):

Canadian Anthology: Canadian Anthology, ed. C. F. Klinck and R. E. Watters, 3rd ed., rev. (1976)

Lit. Hist. Canada: Literary History of Canada, ed. C. F. Klinck; both the 1961 and 1976 edition (3 vols, much revised) are cited, with dates in parentheses.

NCL: New Canadian Library (Toronto, McClelland & Stewart).

Oxf. Compan. (and . . . *Suppl.*): *Oxford Companion to Canadian History and Literature*, and its *Supplement*.

Chapter One

Epigraph: Robertson Davies, "The Northern Muse," *Holiday*, April 1961.

1. *Lit. Hist. Canada* (1961), pp. 82-83.
2. Ibid., p. 81.
3. Ibid., p. 89.
4. Frances Brooke, *Emily Montague* (Toronto: NCL, 1961), pp. 150, 155.
5. Ibid., pp. 166-167
6. *Lit. Hist. Canada* (1961), p. 93.
7. *Canadian Anthology*, p. 19.
8. Ibid., p. 20.
9. Northrop Frye, introduction to *The Stepsure Letters* (Toronto: NCL, 1960), pp. ix, v.
10. Northrop Frye, *The Bush Garden* (Toronto: Anansi, 1971), p. 227.
11. *Lit. Hist. Canada* (1961), p. 110.
12. *Oxf. Compan.*, p. 346.
13. John Moss, *Patterns of Isolation* (Toronto: McClelland & Stewart, 1974), p. 50.
14. *Canadian Anthology*, p. 33.
15. John Richardson, *Wacousta* (Toronto: NCL, 1967), p. xii.
16. Ibid., p. 292.
17. Ibid., p. 105.

Chapter Two

Epigraph: Susanna Strickland Moodie, "A Word for the Novel Writers," *Literary Garland*, August 1851, quoted *Canadian Anthology*, p. 60.
1. *Canadian Anthology*, pp. 50-51.
2. *Lit. Hist. Canada* (1961), p. 100.
3. *Canadian Anthology*, p. 36.
4. Susanna Strickland Moodie, *Roughing It in the Bush* (Toronto: NCL, 1962), intro. by C. F. Klinck, p. xii.
5. Ibid., pp. 151-152.
6. *Canadian Anthology*, p. 29.
7. *Roughing It in the Bush*, pp. 76-77.
8. Wilfred Eggleston, *The Frontier and Canadian Letters* (Toronto: Ryerson, 1957), p. 76.
9. Quoted in E. A. McCourt, *The Canadian West in Fiction*, rev. ed. (Toronto: Ryerson, 1970), pp. 97-98.
10. Ibid., p. 98

Chapter Three

Epigraph: Scott Symons (interview), *Eleven Canadian Novelists*, ed. Graeme Gibson (Toronto: Anansi, 1973), pp. 314-315.
1. *Lit. Hist. Canada* (1961), p. 287.
2. James Kirby, *The Golden Dog* (Toronto: NCL, 1969), p. 127.
3. Ibid., p. 213.
4. Ibid., p. 310.
5. Mary Jane Edwards, ed., *The Evolution of Canadian Literature in English: Beginnings to 1867* (Toronto: Holt, Rinehart & Winston of Canada, 1973), p. 266.
6. *Lit. Hist. Canada* (1961), p. 261.
7. Ibid., p. 113.
8. George Woodcock, "Possessing the Land" in *The Canadian Imagination* (Cambridge, Mass.: Harvard University Press, 1977), pp. 76-77.
9. James DeMille, *A Strange Manuscript Found in a Copper Cylinder* (Toronto: NCL, 1969), p. 113.
10. Ibid., p. 132.
11. Ibid., p. 116.
12. Ibid., pp. 165-166.
13. *Canadian Anthology*, pp. 147-148.
14. Sara Jeannette Duncan, *The Imperialist* (Toronto: NCL, 1961), pp. 232-233.
15. *Canadian Anthology*, story "Little Babiche," p. 171.
16. *Lit. Hist. Canada* (1961), p. 319.

17. Ralph Connor, *The Man from Glengarry* (Toronto: NCL, 1965), p. 20.

18. Ibid., p. x.

19. *Lit. Hist. Canada* (1961), p. 627.

20. Mary Peate, *Girl in a Red River Coat* (Toronto: Clarke, Irwin, 1970), p. 130.

21. Edward William Thomson, *Old Man Savarin Stories* (Toronto: University of Toronto Press, 1974), p. xxii.

22. M. A. Grainger, *Woodsmen of the West* (London: Edward Arnold, 1908), p. 89.

23. Ibid., p. 190.

24. Ibid., p. 205.

25. *Lit. Hist. Canada* (1976), 1: 346: "Writers of Fiction (1880-1920)" by Gordon Roper, S. Ross Beharriell, and Rupert Schieder.

26. *Oxf. Compan.*, p. 255.

27. Stephen Leacock, *Literary Lapses* (Toronto: NCL, 1957), p. 141.

28. Stephen Leacock, *Nonsense Novels* (Toronto: NCL, 1963), p. 54.

29. *Literary Lapses*, p. 95.

30. *Nonsense Novels*, pp. 42-43.

31. Ibid., p. 110.

32. Hugh Hood, *The Swing in the Garden* (Ottawa: Oberon, 1975), pp. 139-140.

33. Stephen Leacock, *Sunshine Sketches of a Little Town* (London: Lane, 1912), Preface, p. xi.

34. Robertson Davies, *A Voice From the Attic* (Toronto: McClelland & Stewart, 1960), pp. 224-225. Davies's book contains other pieces on humor.

Chapter Four

Epigraph: Margaret Laurence (interview), *Eleven Canadian Novelists,* (Toronto, 1973) p. 198.

1. V. B. Rhodenizer, *A Handbook of Canadian Literature* (Ottawa: Graphic, 1930), p. 110.

2. Dick Harrison, *Unnamed Country* (Calgary: University of Alberta Press, 1977), p. 24.

3. Margaret Atwood, *Survival* (Toronto, Anansi, 1972), pp. 122-123.

4. Margaret Stobie, *F. P. Grove* (New York: Twayne, 1973), p. 189.

5. Frederic Niven, *The Flying Years* (Bath: Lythway Press, 1970), pp. 200-201.

6. *Lit. Hist. Canada* (1961), p. 672.

7. Harrison, *Unnamed Country*, p. 131.

8. George Hendrick, *Mazo de la Roche* (New York: Twayne, 1970), p. 136.

9. *Morley Callaghan*, ed. Brandon Conron in *Critical Views on Canadian Writers* (Toronto: McGraw-Hill Ryerson, 1975), p. 32.

10. Morley Callaghan, *The Loved and the Lost* (London: MacGibbon and Kee, 1961), p. 232.

11. Edmund Wilson, *O Canada* (London: Rupert Hart-Davis, 1967), p. 20.

12. D. G. Jones, *Butterfly On Rock* (Toronto: University of Toronto Press, 1970), pp. 51-52.

13. Morley Callaghan, *A Fine and Private Place* (Toronto: Macmillan, 1975), p. 197.

14. Ibid., p. 97.

15. Morley Callaghan, interview No. 16, 1971, *Conversations with Canadian Novelists, Part II* (Toronto: Macmillan, 1973), pp. 31-32.

16. Alec Lucas, *Hugh MacLennan* (Toronto: McClelland & Stewart, 1970), p. 57.

17. Hugh MacLennan, *Barometer Rising* (Toronto: NCL, 1958), p. 153.

18. Wilson, *O Canada*, p. 78.

19. Hugh MacLennan, *Return of the Sphinx* (Toronto: Macmillan, 1971), p. 306.

20. Lucas, *Hugh MacLennan*, p. 47.

21. Ibid., p. 45.

22. Hugh MacLennan, *The Watch That Ends the Night* (Toronto: Macmillan, 1958), pp. 274-275.

23. George Woodcock, *Hugh MacLennan* (Toronto: Copp Clark, 1969), p. 118.

Chapter Five

Epigraph: Raymond Knister, *White Narcissus* (Toronto: NCL, 1962), p. 23.

1. Henry Kreisel, "The Prairie: a State of Mind" in *Canadian Anthology*, p. 626. Originally published in *Transactions of the Royal Society of Canada*, June 1968.

2. Ibid., p. 627.

3. Robert Stead, *The Homesteaders* (Toronto: University of Toronto Press, 1973), p. xix.

4. Raymond Knister, *White Narcissus* (Toronto: NCL, 1962), p. 112.

5. Will R. Bird, *Here Stays Good Yorkshire* (Toronto: Ryerson, 1945), pp. vii-viii.

6. Thomas Raddall, *At the Tide's Turn* (Toronto: NCL, 1959), p. ix.

7. George Ryga, *Ballad of a Stonepicker* (Toronto: Macmillan, 1966), p. 9.

8. Ibid., p. 156.

9. Ernest Buckler, *Ox Bells and Fireflies* (Toronto: NCL, 1974), p. 111.

10. Harrison, *Unnamed Land*, p. 205.

11. Robert Kroetsch, *The Words of My Roaring* (Toronto: Macmillan, 1966), p. 37.

12. Sinclair Ross, *The Lamp at Noon* (Toronto: NCL, 1968), p. 12.

13. McCourt, *Canadian West in Fiction*, p. 101.

14. Irene Baird, *Waste Heritage* (Toronto: Macmillan, 1939), p. 31.

15. Ibid., p. 93.

16. Hugh Garner, *Cabbagetown* (New York: Pocket Books, 1971), preface.

17. Richard Wright, *The Weekend Man* (Toronto: Macmillan, 1970), p. 11.

18. Percy Janes, *The House of Hate* (Toronto: McClelland & Stewart, 1970), p. 320.

19. Joseph Sherman in *Fiddlehead* 96 (Winter 1973): 117.

20. Mordecai Richler, *Cocksure* (New York: Simon & Schuster, 1968), p. 83.

21. *The Sixties: Canadian Writers and Writing of the Decade*, ed. George Woodcock (Vancouver: U. B. C. Publications Centre, 1969), p. 27.

22. George Woodcock, review of *St. Urbain's Horseman*, *Tamarack Review* 58 (1971): 71.

23. Mordecai Richler, *St. Urbain's Horseman* (Toronto: McClelland & Stewart, 1971), p. 464.

24. Hugh Hood, *A Game of Touch* (Don Mills: Longman Canada, 1970), p. 89.

25. Hugh Hood, *The Swing in the Garden* (Ottawa: Oberon, 1975), pp. 83-84.

26. Harry Bruce, interview, *The Narrative Voice* (Toronto: McGraw-Hill Ryerson, 1972), pp. 271-272.

27. James Bacque, *The Lonely Ones* (Toronto: McClelland & Stewart, 1969), p. 173.

Chapter Six

Epigraph: Hugo McPherson in *Literary History of Canada* (1965), p. 720.

1. Paul Hiebert, *Sarah Binks* (Toronto: NCL, 1964), p. 66.

2. Ibid., p. 149.

3. Ibid., pp. 149-150.

4. Earle Birney, *Turvey* (Toronto: NCL, 1963), pp. 98-99.

5. Farley Mowat, *The Boat Who Wouldn't Float* (London: Heinemann, 1970), p. 231.

6. Norman Newton, *The Big Stuffed Hand of Friendship* (Toronto: McClelland & Stewart, 1969), pp. 94-95.

7. James McNamee, *Them Damned Canadians Hanged Louis Riel!* (Toronto: Macmillan, 1971), p. 112.

8. Matt Cohen, *Too Bad Galahad* (Toronto: Coach House Press, 1972), n.p.

9. Alec Lucas, *Peter McArthur* (Boston: Twayne, 1975), p. 120.

Chapter Seven

Epigraph: Gordon Roper, *University of Toronto Quarterly*, Summer 1971.

1. Sandra Esche in *Tamarack Review* 64 (Nov. 1974), p. 85.

2. Dick Harrison, *Unnamed Country*, p. 201; P. L. Surette in *Canadian Fiction Magazine* (Spring 1975), p. 123.

3. W. O. Mitchell, *The Vanishing Point* (Toronto: Macmillan, 1973), p. 385.

4. Alexander Knox, *Night of the White Bear* (Toronto: Macmillan, 1971), pp. 10-11.

5. Ibid., p. 253.

6. James Houston, *The White Dawn* (Don Mills: Longman, 1971), p. 261.

7. Harold Horwood, interview, *Conversations with Canadian Novelists*, pp. 78-79.

8. *Oxf. Compan. Suppl.*, p. 83.

9. Brian Moore, *Judith Hearne* (Boston: Little, Brown, 1956), p. 205.

10. Hallvard Dahlie, *Brian Moore* (Toronto: Copp Clark, 1969), p. 119.

11. Brian Moore, *The Luck of Ginger Coffey* (London: Deutsch, 1962), p. 220.

12. Ibid., p. 157.

13. Ibid., p. 195.

14. Brian Moore, *I Am Mary Dunne* (London: Cape, 1968), pp. 250-251.

15. Atwood, *Survival*, p. 151.

16. *Oxf. Compan. Suppl.*, p. 43.

17. Frederick Ward, *Riverlisp* (Montreal: Tundra Books, 1974), p. 129.

18. Ronald Lee, *Goddam Gypsy* (Montreal: Tundra Books, 1971), p. 236.

19. W. H. New in *Lit. Hist. Canada* (1976), 3: 244.

20. Gwethalyn Graham, *Earth and High Heaven* (Toronto: NCL, 1960), p. 209.

21. Henry Kreisel, *The Rich Man* (Toronto: NCL, 1961), p. 176.

22. A. M. Klein, *The Second Scroll* (Toronto: NCL, 1969), p. 88.

23. Ibid., p. xv.

24. Miriam Waddington, *A. M. Klein* (Toronto: Copp Clark, 1970), p. 103.

25. Atwood, *Survival*, p. 155.
26. George Woodcock, *The Sixties*, p. 52.
27. John Ower, "Sociology, Psychology, and Satire in *The Apprentice-ship of Duddy Kravitz*," *Modern Fiction Studies*, 22, 3 (Autumn 1976): 413.
28. Ibid., p. 423.
29. Ibid., p. 426.
30. *Oxf. Compan. Suppl.*, p. 85.
31. Alice Munro, *Dance of the Happy Shades* (Toronto: Ryerson, 1968), p. viii.
32. W. H. New in *Lit. Hist. Canada* (1976), 3: 257.
33. *Lit. Hist. Canada* (1964), p. 720.
34. *74: New Canadian Stories* (Ottawa: Oberon, 1974), p. 7.
35. Gordon Roper in *University of Toronto Quarterly*, Summer, 1971, p. 387.

Chapter Eight

Epigraph: Donald Cameron, "The Bizarre and the Freaky in Recent Canadian Fiction," in *Canadian Anthology*, p. 644.
1. John Moss, "Invisible Future," *Modern Fiction Studies* 22, 3 (Autumn 1976): 342.
2. George Woodcock, *The Sixties*, p. 122.
3. W. H. New in *Lit. Hist. Canada* (1976), 3: 234.
4. Kent Thompson in *Fiddlehead*, March-April 1970, p. 103.
5. *Fiddlehead*, Winter 1976, p. 113.
6. MacLennan in *The Sixties*, p. 37.
7. Michael Charters, *Victor Victim* (Toronto: Anansi, 1970), p. 146.
8. Richard B. Wright, *In the Middle of a Life* (Toronto: Macmillan, 1973), p. 305.
9. Richard H. Costa, *Malcolm Lowry* (New York: Twayne, 1972), p. 38.
10. Ibid., p. 174.
11. Leonard Cohen, *The Favourite Game* (London: Cape, 1970), pp. 118-119.
12. Ibid., pp. 110-111.
13. Jones, *Butterfly on Rock* (Toronto, 1970), p. 165.
14. *Canadian Anthology*, p. 640.
15. W. H. New in *Lit. Hist. Canada* (1976), 3: 239.
16. Juan Butler, *The Garbageman* (Toronto: Peter Martin Associates, 1972), p. 176.
17. *Eleven Canadian Novelists*, p. 139.
18. Dave Godfrey, *The New Ancestors* (Toronto: New Press, 1972), pp. 195-196.

19. Anthony Boxill, review of *The New Ancestors* in *Fiddlehead* 90 (Summer 1971): 109.

20. Wilson, *O Canada*, pp. 5-6.

21. See *Contemporary Voices*, ed. Donald Stephens (Scarborough, Ont.: Prentice-Hall of Canada, 1972), pp. 152-167.

22. Roberta Rubinstein, "*Surfacing:* Margaret Atwood's Journey to the Interior," *Modern Fiction Studies* 22, 3 (Autumn 1976): 397.

23. Margaret Atwood, *Lady Oracle* (London: Deutsch, 1977), p. 41.

24. Ibid., p. 345.

25. W. H. New in *Lit. Hist. Canada* (1976), 3: 272.

26. Elizabeth Waterston, *Survey* (Toronto: Methuen, 1973), p. 74.

27. P. K. Page, *The Sun and the Moon and Other Fictions* (Toronto: Anansi, 1973), intro., n.p.

28. Emily Carr, *Klee Wyck* (Toronto: Clarke, Irwin, 1971), foreword, n.p.

29. Ronald Sutherland, *Lark des Neiges* (Toronto: New Press, 1971), p. 136.

30. Jane Rule, *Against the Season* (London: P. Davies, 1971), p. 57.

31. Alice Munro, *Lives of Girls and Women* (New York: McGraw-Hill, 1971), p. 77.

32. Clara Thomas, *Margaret Laurence* (Toronto: McClelland & Stewart, 1969), p. 33.

33. Harrison, *Unnamed Country*, p. 192.

34. Quoted in Clara Thomas, p. 42.

35. *The Narrative Voice*, p. 127.

36. Ebbitt Cutler, *The Last Noble Savage* (Montreal: Tundra Books, 1967), p. 6; Beth Harvor, *Women and Children* (Ottawa: Oberon, 1973), p. 59.

37. Dave Godfrey in *Tamarack Review* 48 (1968): 78-79.

38. Norman Levine, *I Don't Want to Know Anyone Too Well* (Toronto: Macmillan, 1971), pp. 35-36.

39. *Oxf. Compan. Suppl.*, p. 112.

40. *Eleven Canadian Novelists*, pp. 79-80.

41. Hugh Hood, *The Swing in the Garden*, p. 94.

42. Brian Moore, *The Great Victorian Collection* (Toronto: McClelland & Stewart, 1975), p. 9.

43. Sheila Watson, *The Double Hook* (Toronto: NCL, 1966), intro., p. 14.

44. Ibid., p. 61.

45. Ibid., p. 119.

46. Ibid., p. 77.

47. Jones, *Butterfly on Rock*, p. 157.

48. Nigel Foxell, *Carnival* (Ottawa: Oberon, 1968), p. 91.

49. James Burke, *The Firefly Hunt* (London: Collins, 1969), p. 171.

50. Russell M. Brown and Donna A. Bennett, "Magnus Eisengrim: the Shadow of the Trickster in the Novels of Robertson Davies," *Modern Fiction Studies* 22, 3 (Autumn 1976), p. 362.

51. John Robert Colombo, *Abracadabra* (Toronto: McClelland & Stewart, 1967), pp. 28-29.

52. John Moss, review of *Scann, Fiddlehead* 96 (Winter 1973): 115.

53. Harry Boyle, *The Great Canadian Novel* (Toronto: Doubleday Canada, 1972), pp. 330-331.

54. George Bowering, *Flycatcher and Other Stories* (Ottawa: Oberon, 1974), p. 97.

Selected Bibliography

GENERAL REFERENCE

Creative Canada, A Biographical Dictionary of Creative and Performing Artists. 2 vols. Toronto: University of Toronto Press, 1971-72. Recent and contemporary figures.

GNAROWSKI, MICHAEL. *A Concise Bibliography of English-Canadian Literature.* Toronto: McClelland & Stewart, 1973. Includes about 50 novelists, to the early 1970s; well-chosen critical references.

KING, BRUCE, ed. *Literatures of the World in English.* London: Routledge & Kegan Paul, 1974. Canada, pp. 42-60.

MOYLES, R. G., comp. *English-Canadian Literature to 1900: A Guide to Information Sources.* Detroit: Gale Research Co., 1976. Preliminary chapters on general reference material as well as later chapters on specific authors.

MYERS, ROBIN, ed. *A Dictionary of Literature in the English Language.* 2 vols. London: Pergamon Press, 1970. Coverage to 1940 only, but useful for earlier figures; volume 2 is an index of titles and authors.

STORY, NORAH, ed. *Oxford Companion to Canadian History and Literature.* Toronto: Oxford University Press, 1967. This, with its 1973 Supplement edited by William Toye, is the best ready reference source available.

VINSON, JAMES, ed. *Contemporary Novelists.* 2nd edition. London: St. James Press, 1976. World coverage with about 600 names, based on recommendations from an extensive panel of advisers.

HISTORICAL AND SOCIAL BACKGROUND

ADAMS, D. K. and RODGERS, H. B. *An Atlas of North American Affairs.* London: Methuen, 1969. Useful for taking a continental view of English-speaking North America; numerous chart-maps.

ADAMS, HOWARD. *Prison of Grass: Canada from the Native Point of View.* Toronto: New Press, 1975. Opinion by, and about, Canadian Indians.

BARTLETT, WILLIAM HENRY. *Bartlett's Canada: A Pre-Confederation Journey.* Texts by Janice Tyrwhitt, introduction by Henry C.

Campbell. Toronto: McClelland & Stewart, 1968. Sketches, sepia drawings, watercolors done by a notable artist in 1838.

BENNET, C. L., CAMPBELL M. W., CLARK, G., FILION, G., and HAIG-BROWN, R. *The Face of Canada*. Toronto: Clarke, Irwin, 1959. Five descriptive essays on major regions, with illustrations.

BOGGS, JEAN SUTHERLAND. *The National Gallery of Canada*. London: Thames and Hudson, 1971. Text with 220 plates.

CUMMING, WILLIAM P., SKELTON, R. A., and QUINN, DAVID B. *The Discovery of North America*. London: Elek, 1971. Continuing text related to quotations from explorers and numerous illustrations.

Expo 67 [commemorative album]. Toronto: Nelson, 1968. An extensive photographic record of the "world's fair" in Montreal, 1967.

GRANT, GEORGE P. *Technology and Empire: Perspectives on North America*. Toronto: Anansi, 1969.

HARPER, J. RUSSELL. *Painting in Canada: A History*. Toronto: University of Toronto/Laval Presses, 1966. A comprehensive survey, generously illustrated.

HORN, MICHAEL, ed. *The Dirty Thirties: Canadians in the Great Depression*. Toronto: Copp Clark, 1972. Articles, newspaper stories, letters and reminiscences, official documents, proposals, contributions by writers, illustrations.

INNIS, MARY QUAYLE, ed. *The Clear Spirit: Twenty Canadian Women and Their Times*. Toronto: University of Toronto Press, 1967. Includes the Strickland sisters, Lucy M. Montgomery, Emily Carr, Mazo de la Roche, and Nellie McClung.

JEFFERYS, C. W. *The Picture Gallery of Canadian History*. 3 vols. Toronto: Ryerson, 1942. Maps, photographs, numerous line drawings.

KILBOURN, WILLIAM, ed. *Canada: A Guide to the Peaceable Kingdom*. Toronto: Macmillan, 1970. Short pieces by public figures, journalists, critics, broadcasters, and artists, including several novelists.

LUMSDEN, IAN, ed. *Close the 49th Parallel Etc.: The Americanization of Canada*. Toronto: University of Toronto Press, 1970. Essays on a wide front, including cultural matters.

LITERARY HISTORY AND CRITICISM

Note: Special attention is directed to entries under *Periodicals* and *Series*. Biographical and critical studies of single authors appear at the end of various author-references in Authors of Fiction, the final section in this list.

ATWOOD, MARGARET. *Survival: A Thematic Guide to Canadian Literature*. Toronto: Anansi, 1972. The author, since publication, has thus far survived a lively trans-Canadian controversy.

BALLSTADT, CARL, ed. *The Search for English–Canadian Literature: an Anthology of Articles from the Nineteenth and Early Twentieth Centuries.* Toronto: University of Toronto Press, 1975. Reprints four essays by Sara Jeannette Duncan as well as Goldwin Smith's "What Is the Matter with Canadian Literature?" which helped fuel a debate at the turn of the century.

BRADBROOK, M. C. *Literature in Action: Studies in Continental and Commonwealth Society.* London: Chatto & Windus, 1972. The chapter on Canada, pp. 153-188, is highly selective but contains interesting social commentary.

EGOFF, SHEILA. *The Republic of Childhood: a Critical Guide to Canadian Children's Literature in English.* Toronto: Oxford, 1967. Attractively arranged and written with insight; discusses the work of some authors who wrote fiction for both children and adults.

GIBSON, GRAEME, ed. *Eleven Canadian Novelists.* Toronto: Anansi, 1973. Interviews, photographs, booklists.

HARRISON, DICK. *Unnamed Country: the Struggle for a Canadian Prairie Fiction.* Toronto: University of Toronto Press, 1977. Blends social and literary history, with considerable attention also to the visual arts.

JONES, D. G. *Butterfly on Rock: A Study of Themes and Images in Canadian Literature.* Toronto: University of Toronto Press, 1970. Luminous exploration, among poems and novels alike, of "the need to make a transition from a garrison culture to one in which the Canadian will feel at home in the world" (p. 7).

KLINCK, CARL F., gen. ed. *Literary History of Canada.* Toronto: University of Toronto Press, 1961; second edition, extensively revised, 3 vols., 1976.

MANDEL, ELI, ed. *Contexts of Canadian Criticism.* Chicago: University of Chicago Press, 1971.

METCALF, JOHN, ed. *The Narrative Voice: Short Stories and Reflections by Canadian Authors.* Toronto: McGraw-Hill Ryerson, 1972. Eleven contemporary writers discuss their work in context.

MOSS, JOHN. *Patterns of Isolation in English Canadian Fiction.* Toronto: McClelland & Stewart, 1974. Thematic discussion in five sections, with detailed exploration of several novels, some in pairs; bibliography.

NEW, WILLIAM H. *Among Worlds: An Introduction to Modern Commonwealth and South African Fiction.* Erin, Ont.: Press Porcepic, 1975. The chapter on Canada, emphasizing international connections, includes comment on French Canadian fiction.

———. *Articulating West.* Toronto: New Press, 1972. A chronicle-critique of recent Canadian fiction with special emphasis on the 1960s.

NIVEN, ALASTAIR, ed. *The Commonwealth Writer Overseas*. Brussels: Didier, 1976. Essays on prairie writing and on language, including one comparing Haliburton with other Commonwealth writers.

PACEY, DESMOND. *A Short History of English-Canadian Literature*. Toronto: Ryerson, 1967. First published in 1952; a highly influential modern survey.

SMITH, A. J. M. *Towards a View of Canadian Letters*. Vancouver: University of British Columbia Press, 1973. Selected critical essays, 1928-1971, chiefly on poetry but occasionally on prose.

SUTHERLAND, RONALD. *Second Image. Comparative Studies in Quebec/ Canadian Literature*. Toronto: New Press, 1971. The principal English-Canadian novelists included are Callaghan, Cohen, Grove, MacLennan, and Mitchell.

WATERSTON, ELIZABETH. *Survey: a Short History of Canadian Literature*. Toronto: Methuen, 1973. Attractively presented in topical form, with abundant quotations and easily identifiable references; extensive "Survey Chart," in three columns, gives historical chronology, Canadian literary events, and literary events elsewhere.

WILSON, EDMUND. *O Canada: An American's Notes on Canadian Culture*. London: Rupert Hart-Davis, 1967 [1964]. Prefaced by an essay on Callaghan; less extended comment on MacLennan and several others.

WOODCOCK, GEORGE, ed. *The Sixties: Canadian Writers and Writing of the Decade*. Vancouver: UBC Publications Centre, 1969. A symposium celebrating the tenth anniversary of the journal *Canadian Literature;* several novelists among the contributors.

SERIES

Canadian Writers: New Canadian Library Originals. Toronto: McClelland & Stewart.
Critical Views on Canadian Writers. Toronto: McGraw-Hill Ryerson.
New Canadian Library. Toronto: McClelland & Stewart.
Studies in Canadian Literature. Toronto, Copp Clark.
Themes in Canadian Literature. Toronto: Macmillan.
Twayne's World Authors Series. Boston: Twayne Publishers.

PERIODICALS (including non-Canadian journals most likely to contain articles of interest on Canadian fiction)

Ariel, Calgary, 1970 +
Canadian Fiction Magazine, Vancouver, 1971 +
Canadian Forum, Toronto, 1920 +
Canadian Literature, Vancouver, 1959 +

Dalhousie Review, Halifax, N.S., 1921+
Fiddlehead, Fredericton, N.B., 1945+
Journal of Canadian Fiction, Montreal, 1972+
Journal of Commonwealth Literature, London, 1965+
Tamarack Review, Toronto, 1956+
University of Toronto Quarterly, Toronto, 1931+
WLWE [World Literature Written in English], Austin [1962–1970] and
    Arlington [1971–1979], Texas—title varies; Guelph, Ontario, 1980 +

ANTHOLOGIES

The Book of Canadian Prose, Vol. 1: *Early Beginnings to Confederation*,
    ed. A.J.M. Smith. Toronto: Gage, 1965.
A Book of Canadian Stories, ed. with introduction by Desmond Pacey.
    Toronto: Ryerson, 1947.
Canadian Anthology, ed. C.F. Klinck and R. E. Watters. 3rd ed., rev.
    Toronto: Gage, 1976.
Canadian Short Stories, second series, ed. Robert Weaver. Toronto:
    Oxford, 1968.
Canadian Stories, ed. Robert Weaver. London/Toronto: Oxford, 1960.
Canadian Winter's Tales, ed. Norman Levine. Toronto: Macmillan,
    1968.
Canadian Writing Today, ed. Mordecai Richler. Harmondsworth: Pen-
    guin, 1970.
Contemporary Voices: the Short Story in Canada, ed. Donald Stephens.
    Scarborough, Ont.: Prentice-Hall of Canada, 1972.
The Depression in Canadian Literature, ed. Alice K. Hale and Sheila
    Brooks. Toronto: Macmillan, 1976.
East of Canada: an Atlantic Anthology, ed. Raymond Fraser, Clyde
    Rose, Jim Stewart. Portugal Cove, Newfoundland: Breakwater
    Books, 1976.
Eskimo Stories from Povungnituk, Quebec [Zebedee Nungak and Eugene
    Arima]. Ottawa: National Museum of Canada, 1969.
✸ *Horizon: Writings of the Canadian Prairie*, ed. Ken Mitchell. Toronto:
    Oxford, 1977.
✓ *Major Canadian Writers*, ed. Desmond Pacey. Toronto: McGraw-Hill
    Ryerson, 1974.
*Marked by the Wild: An Anthology of Literature Shaped by the
    Canadian Wilderness*. Toronto: McClelland & Stewart, 1973.
Modern Canadian Stories, ed. Giose Rimanelli and Roberto Ruberto.
    Toronto: McGraw-Hill Ryerson, 1966.
The Oxford Anthology of Canadian Literature, ed. Robert Weaver and
    William Toye. Toronto: Oxford, 1973.
72 New Canadian Stories. Ottawa: Oberon, 1972 (and later annual
    volumes).

Stories from Ontario, ed. Germaine Warkentin. Toronto: Macmillan, 1974.

Stories from Western Canada, ed. Rudy Wiebe. Toronto: Macmillan, 1972.

Stories of the Outdoors. Vancouver: Mitchell Press, 1970.

AUTHORS OF FICTION

(Arranged alphabetically)

Note: Author's life-dates, when known, are given after names, and biographical studies after the author's book-titles. The lists are selective; only the more important titles are given for most authors; for complete information the reader should consult the biographical studies or other bibliographical guides. When a work has been republished some years after its original appearance, the later edition is usually cited and the date of first publication appears in square brackets at the end of the entry.

ADAMS, IAN. *The Trudeau Papers*. Toronto: McClelland & Stewart, 1971.

ALLEN, GRANT (1848-1899). *The Devil's Die*. New York: F. F. Lowell, 1888.

———. *Philistia*. New York: Harper & Brothers, 1884.

———. *The Woman Who Did*. Boston: Roberts Brothers, 1895.

ALLEN, RALPH (1913-1966). *The Chartered Libertine*. Toronto: Macmillan, 1954.

———. *Home Made Banners*. Toronto: Longmans, 1946.

———. *Peace River Country*. Garden City: Doubleday, 1958.

ASPLER, TONY (b. 1939). *The Streets of Askelon*. London: Secker & Warburg, 1972.

ATWOOD, MARGARET (b. 1939). *The Edible Woman*. London: Deutsch, 1969.

———. *Lady Oracle*. London: Deutsch, 1977.

———. *Surfacing*. London: Deutsch, 1973.

[Interview in *Eleven Canadian Novelists*, ed. Graeme Gibson, Toronto: Anansi, 1973.]

BACQUE, JAMES (b. 1929). *The Lonely Ones*. Toronto: McClelland & Stewart, 1969.

———. *A Man of Talent*. Toronto: New Press, 1972.

[Interview with Milton Wilson in *Creation*, ed. Robert Kroetsch, et al. Toronto: New Press, 1970].

BAILEY, DON. *In the Belly of the Whale*. Ottawa: Oberon, 1974.

BAIRD, IRENE. *The Climate of Power*. Toronto: Macmillan, 1971.

———. *He Rides the Sky*. Toronto: Macmillan, 1941.

———. *John*. Philadelphia, Toronto: Lippincott, 1937.

———. *Waste Heritage*. Toronto: Macmillan, 1974 [1939].

BALLANTYNE, ROBERT M. (1825-1894). *Hudson's Bay; or Life in the Woods of America.* Edinburgh: Blackwood, 1848.

———. *The Young Fur Traders.* Edinburgh: Nimmo, Hay & Mitchell, 1856.

BARBEAU, CHARLES MARIUS (1883-1969). *The Downfall of Temlaham.* Edmonton: Hurtig, 1973 [1928].

BARR, ROBERT (1850-1912). *In the Midst of Alarms.* Philadelphia: Lippincott, 1893.

———. *The Measure of the Rule.* New York: Appleton, 1908 [1906].

BEGG, ALEXANDER (1839-1897). *"Dot It Down."* Toronto: Hunter Rose, 1871.

BELL, DON. *Saturday Night at the Bagel Factory and Other Montreal Stories.* Toronto: McClelland & Stewart, 1972.

BHATIA, JUNE *The Latchkey Kid.* Don Mills: Longman, 1971.

BINDLOSS, HAROLD. (1866-1946). *The Girl from Keller's.* New York: Stokes, 1917.

———. *Ranching for Sylvia.* New York: Stokes, 1913.

BIRD, WILL R. (b. 1891). *Angel Cove* (stories). Toronto: Macmillan, 1972.

———· *Here Stays Good Yorkshire.* Toronto: Ryerson, 1945.

———. *An Earl Must Have a Wife.* Toronto: Clarke, Irwin, 1969.

BIRNEY, EARLE (b. 1904). *Down the Long Table.* Toronto: NCL, 1975 [1955].

———. *Turvey; a Military Picaresque.* Toronto: NCL, 1963 [1949].

[Peter Aichinger, *Earle Birney.* Boston: Twayne, 1979; Frank Davey, *Earle Birney,* 2nd ed. Toronto: Copp Clark, 1974; Bruce Nesbitt, ed., *Earle Birney* (Critical Views on Canadian Writers). Toronto: McGraw-Hill Ryerson, 1974; Richard Robillard, *Earle Birney.* Toronto: NCL, 1971.]

BLAISE, CLARK (b. 1940). *A North American Education.* Toronto: Doubleday Canada, 1973.

BLONDAL, PATRICIA (1927-1959). *A Candle to Light the Sun.* Toronto: McClelland & Stewart, 1960.

———. *From Heaven With a Shout.* Toronto: McClelland & Stewart, 1962.

BODSWORTH, FRED (b. 1918). *The Atonement of Ashley Morden.* New York: Dodd, Mead, 1964.

———. *The Last of the Curlews.* Toronto: NCL, 1963 [1956].

———. *The Sparrow's Fall.* London: Longmans, 1967.

———. *The Strange One.* New York: Dodd, Mead, 1959.

BOWERING, GEORGE (b. 1935). *Flycatcher and Other Stories.* Ottawa: Oberon, 1974.

———. *Mirror on the Floor.* Toronto: McClelland & Stewart, 1967.

[Interview in *Conversations with Canadian Novelists,* ed. Don Cameron. Toronto: Macmillan, 1973.]

BOYLE, HARRY J. (b. 1915). *The Great Canadian Novel*. Toronto: Doubleday Canada, 1972.

———. *Home Brew and Patches*. Toronto: Clarke, Irwin, 1963.

———. *The Luck of the Irish*. Toronto: Macmillan, 1975.

BRAITHWAITE, MAX. *Never Sleep Three in a Bed*. Toronto: McClelland & Stewart, 1969.

———. *The Night We Stole the Mounties' Car*. Toronto: McClelland & Stewart, 1971.

———. *Why Shoot the Teacher?* Toronto: McClelland & Stewart, 1965.

BRANDIS, MARIANNE (b. 1938). *This Spring's Sowing*. Toronto: McClelland & Stewart, 1970.

BRENNAN, ANTHONY. *The Crazy House*. Toronto: McClelland & Stewart, 1975.

BREWSTER, ELIZABETH (b. 1922). *The Sisters*. Ottawa: Oberon, 1974.

BROOKE, FRANCES (1724-1789). *The History of Emily Montague*. Toronto: NCL, 1961 [1769].

BUCKLER, ERNEST (b. 1908). *The Cruelest Month*. Toronto: McClelland & Stewart, 1963.

———. *The Mountain and the Valley*. Toronto: NCL, 1961 [1952].

———. *Ox Bells and Fireflies* (memoir). Toronto: NCL, 1974 [1968].

[Gregory M. Cook, ed., *Ernest Buckler* (Critical Views on Canadian Writers). Toronto: McGraw-Hill Ryerson, 1972. Interview in *Conversations with Canadian Novelists*, ed. Don Cameron. Toronto: Macmillan, 1973.]

BULLOCK, MICHAEL (b. 1918). *Green Beginning: Black Ending* (stories). Vancouver, Sono Nis, 1971.

———. *Sixteen Stories As They Happened*. Vancouver: Sono Nis, 1969.

BURKE, JAMES. *The Firefly Hunt*. London: Collins, 1969.

BUTLER, JUAN (b. 1942). *Cabbagetown Diary: a Documentary*. Toronto: Peter Martin Associates, 1970.

———. *The Garbageman*. Toronto: Peter Martin Associates, 1972.

CALLAGHAN, MORLEY (b. 1903). *It's Never Over*. New York: Scribner, 1930.

———. *The Loved and the Lost*. Toronto: Macmillan, 1951.

———. *The Many Colored Coat*. Toronto: Macmillan, 1960.

———. *More Joy in Heaven*. Toronto: NCL, 1960 [1937].

———. *Morley Callaghan's Stories*. Toronto: Macmillan, 1967.

———. *A Native Argosy*. New York: Scribner, 1929.

———. *Now That April's Here and Other Stories*. New York: Random House, 1936.

———. *Strange Fugitive*. New York: Scribner, 1928.

———. *Such Is My Beloved*. Toronto: NCL, 1957 [1934].

———. *They Shall Inherit the Earth*. Toronto: NCL, 1962 [1935].

[Brandon Conron, *Morley Callaghan*. New York: Twayne, 1966;

Brandon Conron, ed., *Morley Callaghan* (Critical Views on Canadian Writers). Toronto: McGraw-Hill Ryerson, 1975; Victor Hoar, *Morley Callaghan*. Toronto: Copp Clark, 1969. Interview in *Conversations with Canadian Novelists* ed. Don Cameron. Toronto: Macmillan, 1973.]

CARR, EMILY (1871-1945). *The Book of Small*. Toronto: Oxford, 1942.

———. *Growing Pains*. Toronto: Oxford, 1946.

———. *The House of All Sorts*. Toronto: Oxford, 1944.

———. *Klee Wyck*. Toronto: Clarke, Irwin, 1971 [1941].

CHARTERS, MICHAEL (b. 1940). *Victor Victim*. Toronto: Anansi, 1970.

CHILD, PHILIP (b. 1898). *Day of Wrath*. Toronto: Ryerson, 1945.

———. *Mr. Ames Against Time.* Toronto: Ryerson, 1949.

———. *The Village of Souls*. Toronto: Ryerson, 1948 [1933].

CLARKE, AUSTIN C. (b. 1932) *Among Thistles and Thorns*. Toronto: Macmillan, 1965.

———. *The Meeting Point*. Toronto: Macmillan, 1967.

———. *The Survivors of the Crossing*. Toronto: McClelland & Stewart, 1964.

———. *When He Was Free and Young and He Used to Wear Silks* (stories). Toronto: Anansi, 1971.

[Interview in *Eleven Canadian Novelists*, ed. Graeme Gibson. Toronto: Anansi, 1973.]

COHEN, LEONARD (b. 1934). *Beautiful Losers*. Toronto: Bantam, 1971 [1966].

———. *The Favourite Game*. Toronto: NCL, 1970 [1963].

[Michael Gnarowski, ed., *Leonard Cohen* [Critical Views on Canadian Writers]. Toronto: McGraw-Hill Ryerson, 1976; Patricia A. Morley, *The Immoral Moralists: Hugh MacLennan and Leonard Cohen*. Toronto: Clarke, Irwin, 1972; Michael Ondaatje, *Leonard Cohen*. Toronto: NCL, 1970.]

COHEN, MATT (b. 1942). *Columbus and the Fat Lady* (stories). Toronto: Anansi, 1972.

———. *Johnny Crackle Sings*. Toronto: McClelland & Stewart, 1971.

———. *Korsoniloff.* Toronto: Anansi, 1969.

———. *Too Bad Galahad*. Toronto: Coach House Press, 1972.

———. *Wooden Hunters*. Toronto: McClelland & Stewart, 1975.

[Interview in *Eleven Canadian Novelists*, ed. Don Cameron. Toronto: Anansi, 1973.]

CRAVEN, MARGARET. *I Heard the Owl Call My Name*. Toronto: Clarke, Irwin, 1967.

CREIGHTON, LUELLA (b. 1901). *High Bright Buggy Wheels*. New York: Dodd, Mead, 1951.

CUTLER, EBBITT (b. 1923). *The Last Noble Savage*. Montreal: Tundra Books, 1967.

DAVIES, ROBERTSON (b. 1913). *Fifth Business.* Toronto: Macmillan, 1970.
——. *Leaven of Malice.* Toronto: Clarke, Irwin, 1954.
——. *The Manticore.* Toronto: Macmillan, 1972.
——. *A Mixture of Frailties.* Toronto: Macmillan, 1958.
——. *Tempest-Tost.* Toronto: Clarke, Irwin, 1951.
——. *World of Wonders.* New York: Viking, 1975.
[Interview in *Conversations with Canadian Novelists,* ed. Don Cameron. Toronto: Macmillan, 1973.]
DEACON, WILLIAM ARTHUR (b. 1890). *The Four Jameses,* intro. by Doug Fetherling. Toronto: Macmillan, 1974 [1927].
DE LA ROCHE, MAZO (1879-1961). *Jalna.* Boston: Little, Brown, 1927.
——. *Return to Jalna.* Boston: Little, Brown, 1946.
——. *Variable Winds at Jalna.* Toronto: Macmillan, 1954.
——. *Whiteoaks of Jalna.* Boston: Little Brown, 1929.
——. *Young Renny.* Toronto: Macmillan, 1935.
[George Hendrick, *Mazo de la Roche.* New York: Twayne, 1970.]
DE MILLE, JAMES (?1833-1880). *A Strange Manuscript Found in a Copper Cylinder.* Toronto: NCL, 1969 [1888].
DENNIS, CHARLES. *Stoned Cold Soldier.* London: Bachman & Turner, 1973.
DEVINE, J. LLEWELLYN. *The Arrow of Apollyon.* Toronto: McGraw-Hill Ryerson, 1971.
DUNCAN, SARA JEANNETTE (1862-1922). *An American Girl in London.* London: Chatto & Windus, 1891.
——. *Cousin Cinderella: a Canadian Girl in London.* Toronto: Macmillan, 1908.
——. *The Imperialist.* Toronto: NCL, 1961 [1904].
——. *The Simple Adventures of a Memsahib.* New York: Appleton, 1893.
——. *A Voyage of Consolation.* London: Methuen, 1898.
EGGLESTON, WILFRED (b. 1901). *The High Plains.* Toronto: Macmillan, 1938.
ENGEL, MARIAN (b. 1933). *Bear.* London: Routledge & Kegan Paul, 1977.
——. *The Honeymoon Festival.* Toronto: Anansi, 1970.
——. *No Clouds of Glory.* Don Mills: Longman, 1968.
[Interview in *Eleven Canadian Novelists,* ed. Graeme Gibson. Toronto: Anansi, 1973.]
EVANS, CECILY LOUISE. *Nemesis.* Toronto: Doubleday, 1970.
——. *The Newel Post.* Toronto: Doubleday, 1967.
EVANS, HUBERT R. *The Mist on the River.* Toronto: Copp Clark, 1955.
FIELDEN, CHARLOTTE. *Crying As She Ran.* Toronto: Macmillan, 1970.
FINDLEY, TIMOTHY (b. 1931). *The Butterfly Plague.* New York: Viking, 1969.
——. *The Last of the Crazy People.* Don Mills: General, 1967.

[Interviews in *Conversations with Canadian Novelists*, ed. Don Cameron (Toronto: Macmillan, 1973), and *Eleven Canadian Novelists*, ed. Graeme Gibson. Toronto: Anansi, 1973.]

FORER, MORT (b. 1922). *The Humback*. Toronto: McClelland & Stewart, 1969.

FOXELL, NIGEL. *Carnival*. Ottawa: Oberon, 1968.

————. *Schoolboy Rising*. Ottawa: Oberon, 1973.

FRANKLIN, STEPHEN (b. 1922). *Knowledge Park*. Toronto: McClelland & Stewart, 1972.

FRASER, SYLVIA.. *The Candy Factory*. Toronto: McClelland & Stewart, 1975.

————. *Pandora*. Toronto: NCL, 1972.

FRY, ALAN (b. 1931). *Come a Long Journey*. Toronto: Doubleday, 1971.

GALLANT, MAVIS (b. 1922). *The End of the World and Other Stories*. Toronto: NCL, 1974.

————. *A Fairly Good Time*. New York: Random House, 1970.

————. *Green Water, Green Sky: a Novel in Which Time is the Principal Actor*. Boston: Houghton Mifflin, 1969.

————. *My Heart is Broken* (stories). Don Mills: PaperJacks, 1974 [1964].

————. *The Other Paris* (stories). Boston: Houghton Mifflin, 1966.

————. *The Pegnitz Junction*. New York: Random House, 1973.

GALT, JOHN (1779-1839). *Bogle Corbet; or the Emigrants*. London: Colburn & Bentley, 1831.

————. *Lawrie Todd; or, the Settlers in the Woods*. New York: Harper, 1830.

GARBER, LAWRENCE. *Circuit* (stories). Toronto: Anansi, 1970.

GARNER, HUGH (b. 1913). *Cabbagetown*. New York: Simon & Schuster, 1971 [1963].

————. *Hugh Garner's Best Stories*. New York: Simon & Schuster, 1971 [1963].

————. *A Nice Place to Visit*. Toronto: Ryerson, 1970.

————. *The Sin Sniper*. New York: Simon & Schuster, 1970.

————. *Storm Below*. New York: Simon & Schuster, 1971 [1949].

————. *Violation of the Virgins* (stories). Toronto: McGraw-Hill Ryerson, 1971.

GIBSON, GRAEME (b. 1934). *Communion*. Toronto: Anansi, 1971.

————. *Five Legs*. Toronto: Anansi, 1969.

GLASS, JOANNA M. (b. 1936). *Reflections on a Mountain Summer*. Toronto: McClelland & Stewart, 1974.

GODFREY, DAVE (b. 1938). *Death Goes Better with Coca-Cola*. Erin, Ont.: Press Porcépic, 1973 [1967].

————. *The New Ancestors*. Toronto: New Press, 1970.

[Interviews in *Conversations with Canadian Novelists*, ed. Don

Cameron (Toronto: Macmillan, 1973), and *Eleven Canadian Novelists*, ed. Graeme Gibson (Toronto: Anasi, 1973).]

GORDON, CHARLES WILLIAM [Ralph Connor] (1860-1937). *Black Rock: a Tale of the Selkirks*. Toronto: Westminster, 1898.

———. *The Foreigner: a Tale of Saskatchewan*. Toronto: Westminster, 1909.

———. *Glengarry School Days: a Story of the Early Days in Glengarry*. Chicago: Revell, 1902.

———. *The Man from Glengarry: a Tale of the Ottawa*. Toronto: NCL, 1969 [1901].

———. *The Sky Pilot: a Tale of the Foothills*. Chicago: Revell, 1899. ⁷

GRAHAM, GWETHALYN (1913-1965). *Earth and High Heaven*. Toronto: NCL, 1960 [1944].

GRAINGER, MARTIN ALLERDALE (1874-1941). *Woodsmen of the West*. London: Edward Arnold, 1908.

GRAY, SIMON. *Colmain*. London: Faber, 1963.

———. *Little Portia*. London: Faber, 1967.

———. *Simple People*. London: Faber, 1965.

GROVE, FREDERICK PHILIP (1871-1948). *Consider Her Ways*. Toronto: Macmillan, 1947.

———. *Fruits of the Earth*. Toronto: NCL, 1965 [1933]. ♭

———. *In Search of Myself*. Toronto: Macmillan, 1946.

———. *It Needs to Be Said*. Toronto: Macmillan, 1929.

———. *The Master of the Mill*. Toronto: NCL, 1961 [1944].

———. *Our Daily Bread*. Toronto: Macmillan, 1928.

———. *Over Prairie Trails*. Toronto: NCL, 1957 [1922]. ✓

———. *A Search for America*. Toronto: NCL, 1971 [1927]. ⊘

———. *Settlers of the Marsh*. Toronto: NCL, 1966 [1925]. ⌐

———. *Tales from the Margin*, ed. Desmond Pacey. Toronto: Ryerson, 1971.

———. *The Turn of the Year*. Toronto: McClelland & Stewart, 1923.

———. *Two Generations*. Toronto: Ryerson, 1939.

[Joan Hind-Smith, *Three Voices*. Toronto: Clarke, Irwin, 1975; Desmond Pacey, ed., *F. P. Grove* (Critical Views on Canadian Writers). Toronto: McGraw-Hill Ryerson, 1970; Douglas O. Spettigue, *Frederick Philip Grove*. Toronto: Copp Clark, 1969; Douglas O. Spettigue, *FPG: The European Years*. Ottawa: Oberon, 1973; ⁕ Margaret Stobie, *F. P. Grove*. New York: Twayne, 1973; Ronald Sutherland, *Frederick Philip Grove*. Toronto: NCL, 1969.]

HALIBURTON, THOMAS CHANDLER (1796-1865). *The Clockmaker*. Toronto: NCL, 1958 [1836]. ◇

———. *The Letter Bag of the Great Western*. London: Bentley, 1840.

———. *The Sam Slick Anthology*, ed. W. S. Avis, intro. by R. E. Watters. Toronto: Clarke, Irwin, 1969.

————. *Traits of American Humor,* by Native Authors. London: Colburn, 1852.

HARCOURT, PALMA. *Climate for Conspiracy.* London: Collins, 1974.

HARLOW, ROBERT (b. 1923). *A Gift of Echoes.* Toronto: Macmillan, 1965.

————. *Royal Murdoch.* Toronto: Macmillan, 1962.

————. *Scann.* Vancouver: Sono Nis, 1972.

HART, JULIA CATHERINE (1796-1867). *St. Ursula's Convent; or, the Nun of Canada.* Kingston: Thomson, 1824.

————. *Tonnewonte; or the Adopted Son of America.* Watertown, N.Y.: Exeter, Meder, 1831.

HARVOR, BETH. *Women and Children.* Ottawa: Oberon, 1973.

HELWIG, DAVID (b. 1938). *The Day Before Tomorrow.* Ottawa: Oberon, 1971.

————. *The Glass Knight.* Ottawa: Oberon, 1976.

————. *The Streets of Summer.* Ottawa: Oberon, 1969.

————. "Time in Fiction" in *The Narrative Voice,* ed. J. Metcalf. Toronto: McGraw-Hill Ryerson, 1972.

HIEBERT, PAUL G. (b. 1892). *Sarah Binks.* Toronto: NCL, 1964 [1947].

————. *Willows Revisited.* Toronto: McClelland & Stewart, 1967.

HINDMARSH, GLADYS. *The Peter Stories.* Toronto: Coach House Press, 1976.

HOOD, HUGH (b. 1928). *Around the Mountain: Scenes from Montreal Life* (stories). Toronto: Peter Martin Associates, 1967.

————. *The Camera Always Lies.* (New York: Harcourt, Brace, World, 1967.

————. *Flying a Red Kite* (stories). Toronto: McGraw-Hill Ryerson, 1967 [1962].

————. *The Fruit Man, the Meat Man, and the Manager* (stories). Ottawa: Oberon, 1971.

————. *A Game of Touch.* Don Mills: Longman Canada, 1970.

————. *The Swing in the Garden.* Ottawa: Oberon, 1975.

————. *White Figure, White Ground.* Toronto: Ryerson, 1964.

————. *You Can't Get There from Here.* Ottawa: Oberon, 1972.

[Essay by Hood in *The Narrative Voice,* ed. J. Metcalf (Toronto: McGraw-Hill Ryerson, 1972); Patricia Morley, *The Comedians: Hugh Hood and Rudy Wiebe.* (Toronto: Clarke, Irwin, 1977).]

HORWOOD, HAROLD (b. 1923). *Tomorrow Will Be Sunday.* New York: Doubleday, 1966.

————. *White Eskimo.* Toronto: Doubleday, 1972.

[Interview in *Conversations with Canadian Novelists,* ed. Don Cameron. Toronto: Macmillan, 1973.]

HOUSTON, JAMES. *The White Dawn.* Don Mills: Longman, 1971.

HOWARD, BLANCHE. *The Manipulator.* Toronto: McClelland & Stewart, 1972.

HUNTER, ROBERT (b. 1941). *Erebus.* Toronto: McClelland & Stewart, 1968.

JACOT, MICHAEL. *The Last Butterfly.* Toronto: McClelland & Stewart, 1973.

JANES, PERCY. *House of Hate.* Toronto: McClelland & Stewart, 1970.

KIRBY, JAMES (1817-1906). *The Golden Dog.* Toronto: NCL, 1969 [1887].

KLEIN, ABRAHAM MOSES (1909-1972). *The Second Scroll.* Toronto: NCL, 1969 [1951].

[Tom Marshall, ed. *A. M. Klein* (Critical Views on Canadian Writers), Toronto: McGraw-Hill Ryerson, 1970; Miriam Waddington, *A. M. Klein,* 2nd. ed. Toronto: Copp Clark, 1974.]

KNIGHT, DAVID. *Farquharson's Physique and What It Did to His Mind.* New York: Stein and Day, 1970.

KNISTER, RAYMOND (1899-1932). *Selected Stories,* ed. with intro. by Michael Gnarowski. Ottawa: University of Ottawa Press, 1972.

———. *White Narcissus.* Toronto: NCL, 1962 [1929].

KNOX, ALEXANDER (b. 1907). *Bride of Quietness.* Toronto: Macmillan, 1933.

———. *Night of the White Bear.* Toronto: Macmillan, 1971.

KOCH, ERIC. *The French Kiss.* Toronto: McClelland & Stewart, 1969.

———. *The Leisure Riots.* Montreal: Tundra Books, 1973.

KREISEL, HENRY (b. 1922). *The Betrayal.* Toronto: McClelland & Stewart, 1964.

———. *The Rich Man.* Toronto: NCL, 1961 [1948].

KROETSCH, ROBERT (b. 1927). *But We Are Exiles.* Toronto: Macmillan, 1965.

———. *Gone Indian.* Toronto: New Press, 1973.

———. *The Studhorse Man.* Toronto: Macmillan, 1969.

———. *The Words of My Roaring.* Toronto: Macmillan, 1966.

[Interview in *Conversations with Canadian Novelists,* ed. Don Cameron. Toronto: Macmillan, 1973.]

LADOO, HAROLD SONNY (b. 1945). *No Pain Like This Body.* Toronto: Anasi, 1972.

LAURENCE, MARGARET (b. 1926). *A Bird in the House* (stories). Toronto: McClelland & Stewart, 1970.

———. *The Diviners.* Toronto: McClelland & Stewart, 1974.

———. *The Fire-Dwellers.* Toronto: McClelland & Stewart, 1969.

———. *A Jest of God.* Toronto: McClelland & Stewart, 1966.

———. *The Stone Angel.* Toronto: NCL, 1968 [1964].

———. *This Side Jordan.* Toronto: McClelland & Stewart, 1960.

———. *The Tomorrow-tamer* (stories). Toronto: NCL, 1970 [1963].

[Essay by Laurence in *The Narrative Voice,* ed. J. Metcalf (Toronto: McGraw-Hill Ryerson, 1972); Joan Hind Smith, *Three Voices.* Toronto: Clarke, Irwin, 1975; interviews in *Conversations with*

Canadian Novelists, ed. Don Cameron (Toronto: Macmillan, 1973) and *Eleven Canadian Novelists,* ed. Graeme Gibson (Toronto: Anansi, 1973); William New, ed., *Margaret Laurence* (Critical Views on Canadian Writers). Toronto: McGraw-Hill Ryerson, 1977; Clara Thomas, *Margaret Laurence.* Toronto: NCL, 1969; Clara Thomas, *The Manawaka World of Margaret Laurence.* Toronto: NCL, 1976.]

LAURISTON, VICTOR *Inglorious Milton.* Chatham: Tiny Tree Club, 1934.

LEACOCK, STEPHEN (1869-1944). *Literary Lapses.* Toronto: NCL, 1957 [1910].

———. *Nonsense Novels.* Toronto: NCL, 1963 [1911].

———. *Sunshine Sketches of a Little Town.* Toronto: NCL, 1948 [1912]. [Donald Cameron, *Faces of Leacock.* Toronto: McGraw-Hill Ryerson, 1976; Robertson Davies, *Stephen Leacock.* Toronto: NCL, 1970; Stephen Franklin, *Leacock.* Toronto: Clarke, Irwin, 1970; Elizabeth Kimball, *The Man in the Panama Hat.* Toronto: McClelland & Stewart, 1970.]

LEE, RONALD (b. 1934). *Goddam Gypsy, an Autobiographical Novel.* Montreal: Tundra Books, 1971.

LE PAN, DOUGLAS (b. 1914). *The Deserter.* Toronto: McClelland & Stewart, 1964.

LEVINE, NORMAN (b. 1924). *The Angled Road.* London: Laurie, 1952.

———. *Canada Made Me.* London: Putnam, 1958.

———. *From a Seaside Town.* Toronto: Macmillan, 1970.

———. *I Don't Want to Know Anyone Too Well and Other Stories.* Toronto: Macmillan, 1971.

———. *One Way Ticket* (stories). London: Secker & Warburg, 1961.

LOWRY, MALCOLM (1909-1957). *Dark As the Grave Wherein My Friend Is Laid.* Don Mills: General, 1968.

———. *Hear Us O Lord from Heaven Thy Dwelling Place.* Toronto: McClelland & Stewart, 1961.

———. *Lunar Caustic.* London: Cape, 1968.

———. *October Ferry to Gabriola.* New York: World, 1970.

———. *Ultramarine.* London: Cape, 1933.

———. *Under the Volcano.* Harmondsworth: Penguin, 1962 [1947]. [Richard H. Costa, *Malcolm Lowry.* New York: Twayne, 1972; Tony Kilgallin, *Lowry.* Erin, Ont.: Porcépic Press, 1973; William New, *Malcolm Lowry.* Toronto: NCL, 1971.]

LUDWIG, JACK (b. 1922). *Above Ground.* Boston: Little, Brown, 1968.

———. *Confusions.* Toronto: McClelland & Stewart, 1963. [Interviews in *Conversations with Canadian Novelists,* ed. Don Cameron. Toronto: Macmillan, 1973; and *Eleven Canadian Novelists,* ed. Graeme Gibson Toronto: Anansi, 1973.]

MCARTHUR, PETER (1866-1924). *The Ghost and the Burglar.* New York: McArthur & Ryder, 1905.

———. *The Peacemakers.* New York: McArthur & Ryder, 1905.
[Alec Lucas. *Peter McArthur.* Boston: Twayne, 1975.]
MACBETH, MADGE (1878-1965). *The Kinder Bees.* London: L. Dickson, 1935.
———. *The Land of Afternoon.* Ottawa: Graphic, 1924.
McCLUNG, NELLIE M. (1873-1951). *The Black Creek Stopping-House and Other Stories.* Toronto: Briggs, 1912.
———. *The Second Chance.* New York: Doubleday, 1910.
———. *Sowing Seeds in Danny.* New York: Doubleday, 1908.
McCULLOCH, THOMAS (1777-1843). *The Stepsure Letters.* Toronto: NCL, 1960 [1821-22].
McDOUGALL, COLIN. *Execution.* Toronto: Macmillan, 1958.
McEWEN, GWENDOLYN (b. 1941). *Julian the Magician.* Toronto: Macmillan, 1963.
———. *King of Egypt, King of Dreams.* Toronto: Macmillan, 1971.
———. *Noman* (stories). Ottawa: Oberon, 1972.
MACLENNAN, HUGH (b. 1907). *Barometer Rising.* Toronto: NCL, 1958 [1941].
———. *Each Man's Son.* Toronto: NCL, 1962 [1951].
———. *The Precipice.* Toronto: Collins, 1948.
———. *Return of the Sphinx.* Toronto: Macmillan, 1967.
———. *Two Solitudes.* New York: Duell, Sloan, 1945.
———. *The Watch That Ends the Night.* Toronto: Macmillan, 1958.
[Robert H. Cockburn, *The Novels of Hugh MacLennan.* Montreal: Harvest House, 1970; Paul Goetsch, ed., *Hugh MacLennan* (Critical Views on Canadian Writers). Toronto: McGraw-Hill Ryerson, 1973; interview in *Conversations with Canadian Novelists*, ed. Don Cameron. Toronto: Macmillan, 1973; Alec Lucas, *Hugh MacLennan.* Toronto: NCL, 1970; Patricia A. Morley, *The Immoral Moralists: Hugh MacLennan and Leonard Cohen.* Toronto: Clarke, Irwin, 1972; George Woodcock, *Hugh MacLennan.* Toronto: Copp Clark, 1969.]
MACLEOD, CHARLOTTE. *Brass Pounder.* Boston: Little, Brown, 1971.
McNAMEE, JAMES (b. 1904). *Them Damned Canadians Hanged Louis Riel!* Toronto: Macmillan, 1971.
McWHIRTER, GEORGE. *Bodyworks.* Ottawa: Oberon, 1974.
MARKOOSIE (b. 1943). *Harpoon of the Hunter.* Montreal: McGill-Queen's University Press, 1970.
MARSHALL, JOYCE (b. 1913). *Lovers and Strangers.* Philadelphia: Lippincott, 1957.
———. *Presently Tomorrow.* Boston: Little, Brown, 1946.
———. *A Private Place* (stories). Ottawa: Oberon, 1975.
METCALFE, JOHN (b. 1938). *Going Down Slow.* Toronto: McClelland & Stewart, 1972.
———. *The Lady Who Sold Furniture* (stories). Toronto: Clarke, Irwin, 1970.

———. *The Teeth of My Father* (stories). Ottawa: Oberon, 1975.
[Essay by Metcalf in *The Narrative Voice*, ed. J. Metcalf. Toronto: McGraw-Hill Ryerson, 1972.]
MILLS, JOHN (b. 1930). *The Land of Is*. Ottawa: Oberon, 1973.
———. *October Man*. Ottawa: Oberon, 1973.
MITCHELL, WILLIAM ORMOND (b. 1914). *Jake and the Kid*. Toronto: Macmillan, 1961.
———. *The Kite*. Toronto: Macmillan, 1962.
———. *The Vanishing Point*. Toronto: Macmillan, 1973.
———. *Who Has Seen the Wind?* Toronto: Macmillan, 1960 [1947].
[Interview in *Conversations with Canadian Novelists*, ed. Don Cameron. Toronto: Macmillan, 1973.]
MONTGOMERY, LUCY MAUDE (1877-1942). *Anne of Green Gables*. Boston: Page, 1908.
———. *Anne of Avonlea*. Boston: Page, 1909.
MOODIE, SUSANNA STRICKLAND (1803-1889). *Geoffrey Monckton; or, the Faithless Guardian*. New York: DeWitt & Davenport, 1855. London, 1856, as *The Moncktons*.
———. *Life in the Clearings*. Toronto: Macmillan, 1959 [1853].
———. *Mark Hurdlestone, the Gold Worshipper*. London: Bentley, 1853.
———. *Roughing It in the Bush*. Toronto: NCL, 1962 [1852].
[Carol Shields, *Susanna Moodie, Voice and Vision*. Ottawa: Borealis, 1977.]
MOORE, BRIAN (b. 1921). *An Answer from Limbo*. Boston: Little, Brown, 1962.
———. *The Emperor of Ice Cream*. Toronto: McClelland & Stewart, 1965.
———. *The Feast of Lupercal*. Boston: Little, Brown, 1957.
———. *Fergus*. Toronto: McClelland & Stewart, 1970.
———. *The Great Victorian Collection*. Toronto: McClelland & Stewart, 1975.
———. *I Am Mary Dunne*. Toronto: NCL, 1976 [1966].
———. *Judith Hearne*. Toronto: NCL, 1964 [1956].
———. *The Luck of Ginger Coffey*. Toronto: NCL, 1972 [1960].
———. *The Revolution Script*. London: Cape, 1972.
[Hallvard Dahlie, *Brian Moore*. Toronto: Copp Clark, 1969; Interview in *Conversations with Canadian Novelists*, ed. Don Cameron. Toronto: Macmillan, 1973.]
MOWAT, FARLEY. *The Boat Who Wouldn't Float*. London: Heinemann, 1970.
[Alec Lucas, *Farley Mowat*. Toronto: NCL, 1976.]
MUNRO, ALICE (b. 1931). *Dance of the Happy Shades*. Toronto: McGraw-Hill Ryerson, 1968.
———. *Lives of Girls and Women*. New York: McGraw-Hill, 1971.

―――. *Something I've Been Meaning To Tell You.* Toronto: McGraw-Hill Ryerson, 1974.

[Essay by Munro in *The Narrative Voice,* ed. J. Metcalf. Toronto: McGraw-Hill Ryerson, 1973; interview in *Eleven Canadian Novelists,* ed. Graeme Gibson. Toronto: Anansi, 1973.]

MYERS, MARTIN (b. 1927). *The Assignment.* New York: Harper & Row, 1971.

[Interview in *Conversations with Canadian Novelists,* ed. Don Cameron. Toronto: Macmillan, 1973.]

NEWMAN, C. J. (b. 1935). *We Always Take Care of Our Own.* London: Gollancz, 1965.

NEWTON, NORMAN (b. 1929). *The Big Stuffed Hand of Friendship.* Toronto: McClelland & Stewart, 1969.

―――. *The House of Gods.* London: P. Owen, 1961.

―――. *The One True Man.* Toronto: McClelland & Stewart, 1963.

NICHOL, B. P. (b. 1944). *Two Novels: Andy* and *For Jesus Lunatick.* Toronto: Coach House Press, 1971.

NICHOLS, RUTH (b. 1948). *The Ceremony of Innocence.* London: Faber, 1969.

NOWLAN, ALDEN (b. 1933). *Miracle of Indian River* (stories). Toronto: Clarke, Irwin, 1968.

―――. *Various Persons Named Kevin O'Brien.* Toronto: Clarke, Irwin, 1973.

O'HAGAN, HOWARD. *Tay John.* New York: C. N. Potter, 1960 [1939].

OSTENSO, MARTHA (1900-1963). *Wild Geese.* Toronto: NCL, 1971 [1925].

PACEY, DESMOND (1917-1975). *Waken, Lords and Ladies Gay* (stories). Ottawa: University of Ottawa Press, 1974.

PAGE, PATRICIA K. (b. 1916). *The Sun and the Moon and Other Fictions.* Toronto: Anansi, 1973 [1944].

PARKER, GILBERT (1860-1932). *Pierre and His People: Tales of the Far North.* London: Methuen, 1892.

―――. *The Seats of the Mighty.* London: Methuen, 1896.

―――. *Tarpec.* New York: Harper, 1927.

―――. *The Trespasser.* New York: Appleton, 1893.

―――. *Works,* Imperial ed., 23 vols. New York: Scribner, 1912-23.

PEATE, MARY (b. 1929). *Girl in a Red River Coat.* Toronto: Clarke, Irwin, 1970.

PETER, JOHN. *Along That Coast.* Toronto: Doubleday, 1964.

―――. *Runaway.* Toronto: Doubleday, 1969.

―――. *Shake Hands at Winter.* Toronto: Doubleday, 1967.

PETERSON, LEN (b. 1917). *Chipmunk.* Toronto: McClelland & Stewart, 1949.

POWE, BRUCE [ELLIS PORTAL] (b. 1925). *Killing Ground, the Canadian Civil War.* Toronto: Peter Martin Associates, 1968.

RADDALL, THOMAS H. (b. 1903). *At the Tide's Turn and Other Stories.* Toronto: NCL, 1959.

————. *His Majesty's Yankees*. Garden City: Doubleday, 1942.

————. *The Nymph and the Lamp*. Toronto: NCL, 1963 [1950].

————. *The Pied Piper of Dipper Creek and Other Tales*. Edinburgh: Blackwood, 1938.

————. *Tidefall*. Toronto: McClelland & Stewart, 1953.

————. *The Wings of Night*. Toronto: Doubleday, 1963 [1956].

[Interview in *Conversations with Canadian Novelists*, ed. Don Cameron. Toronto: Macmillan, 1973.]

RICHARDS, DAVID ALLEN. *Blood Ties*. Ottawa: Oberon, 1976.

————. *The Coming of Winter*. Ottawa: Oberon, 1974.

RICHARDSON, JOHN (1796-1852). *The Canadian Brothers; or, The Prophecy Fulfilled*. Montreal: Armour & Ramsey, 1840.

————. *Écarté; or, The Salons of Paris*. London: Colburn, 1829.

————. *Wacousta; or, The Prophecy*. Toronto: NCL, 1967 [1832].

RICHLER, MORDECAI (b. 1939). *The Acrobats*. London: Deutsch, 1954.

————. *The Apprenticeship of Duddy Kravitz*. Toronto: NCL 1969 [1959].

————. *A Choice of Enemies*. London: Deutsch, 1957.

————. *Cocksure*. Toronto: McClelland & Stewart, 1968.

————. *The Incomparable Atuk*. Toronto: NCL, 1971 [1963].

————. *St. Urbain's Horseman*. Toronto: McClelland & Stewart, 1971.

————. *Son of a Smaller Hero*. Toronto: NCL, 1966 [1957].

[Interviews in *Conversations with Canadian Novelists*, ed. Don Cameron. Toronto: Macmillan, 1973, and *Eleven Canadian Novelists*, ed. Graeme Gibson. Toronto: Anansi, 1973. G. David Sheps, ed. *Mordecai Richler* (Critical Views on Canadian Writers). Toronto: McGraw-Hill Ryerson, 1971; George Woodcock, *Mordecai Richler*. Toronto: NCL, 1970.]

RIIS, SHARON, *The True Story of Ida Johnson*. Toronto: Canadian Women's Educational Press, 1977.

ROBERTS, CHARLES G. D. (1860-1943). *Earth's Enigmas*. Boston: Lamson Wolffe, 1896.

————. *The Kindred of the Wild*. Boston: Page, 1902.

[W. J. KEITH, *Charles G. D. Roberts*. Toronto: Copp Clark, 1969.]

ROHMER, RICHARD. *Exodus/UK*. Toronto: McClelland & Stewart, 1975.

————. *Exxoneration*. Toronto: McClelland & Stewart, 1974.

————. *Ultimatum*. Toronto: Clarke, Irwin, 1973.

ROSS, SINCLAIR (b. 1908). *As For Me and My House*. Toronto: NCL, 1957 [1941].

————. *The Lamp at Noon and Other Stories*. Toronto: NCL, 1968.

————. *Sawbones Memorial*. Toronto: NCL, 1978 [1974].

————. *The Well*. Toronto: Macmillan, 1958.

————. *A Whir of Gold*. Toronto: McClelland & Stewart, 1970.

[Lorraine McMullen, *Sinclair Ross*. Boston: Twayne, 1979.]

RULE, JANE (b. 1931). *Against the Season*. London: P. Davies, 1971.
———. *The Desert of the Heart*. Toronto: Macmillan, 1964.
———. *Theme for Diverse Instruments*. Vancouver: Talonbooks, 1973.
———. *This Is Not for You*. New York: McCall, 1970.
RYGA, GEORGE (b. 1932). *Ballad of a Stone-Picker*. Toronto: Macmillan, 1966.
———. *Hungry Hills*. Vancouver: Talonbooks, 1974.
SALVERSON, LAURA G. (b. 1890). *Confessions of an Immigrant's Daughter*. London: Faber, 1939.
———. *The Dark Weaver*. Toronto: Ryerson, 1937.
———. *The Viking Heart*. New York: Doran, 1923.
SAUNDERS, MARGARET MARSHALL (1861-1947). *Beautiful Joe*. Philadelphia: American Baptist Publishing Society, 1894.
SCHROEDER, ANDREAS (b. 1946). *The Late Man*. Vancouver: Sono Nis, 1972.
SCHULL, JOSEPH. *The Jinker*. Toronto: Macmillan, 1968.
SCOTT, CHRIS. *Bartleby*. Toronto: Anansi, 1971.
SCOTT, DUNCAN CAMPBELL (1862-1947). *In the Village of Viger*. Boston: Copeland Day, 1896.
———. *The Witching of Elspie* (stories). New York: Doran, 1923.
SHAPIRO, LIONEL. *The Sealed Verdict*. New York: Doubleday, 1947.
———. *The Sixth of June*. New York: Doubleday, 1955.
SMITH, RAY. *Cape Breton is the Thought Control Centre of Canada* (stories). Toronto: Anansi, 1969.
[Essay by Smith in *The Narrative Voice*, ed. J. Metcalf. Toronto: McGraw-Hill Ryerson, 1972.]
STEAD, ROBERT J. C. (1880-1959). *Grain*. Toronto: McClelland & Stewart, 1926.
———. *The Homesteaders*. Toronto: University of Toronto Press, 1973 [1916].
STEFANYK, VASYL (1871-1935). *The Stone Cross* (stories), trans. from Ukrainian by Joseph Wiznuk and C. H. Andrusyshen. Toronto: McClelland & Stewart, 1971.
STEIN, DAVID LEWIS (b. 1937). *My Sexual and Other Revolutions: the Memoirs of Daniel Johnson*. Toronto: New Press, 1971.
———. *Scratch One Dreamer*. Toronto: McClelland & Stewart, 1967.
[Interview in *Conversation with Canadian Novelists*, ed. Don Cameron. Toronto: Macmillan, 1973.]
STRINGER, ARTHUR J. A. (1874-1950). *Prairie Stories*. New York: Burt, 1936.
SUCH, PETER (b. 1939). *Fallout*. Toronto: Anansi, 1969.
———. *Riverrun*. Toronto: Clarke, Irwin, 1973.
SUMMERS, MERNA. *The Skating Party* (stories). Ottawa: Oberon, 1974.
SUTHERLAND, RONALD (b. 1933). *Lark des Neiges*. Toronto: New Press, 1971.

SYMONS, R. D. *The Broken Snare, the Story of a Frontier Family.*
Toronto: Doubleday, 1970.
————. *Still the Wind Blows: a Historical Novel of the Northwest 1860-
1916.* Saskatoon: Prairie Books, 1971.
SYMONS, SCOTT (b. 1933). *Combat Journal of Place d'Armes.* Toronto:
McClelland & Stewart, 1967.
[Interview in *Eleven Canadian Novelists,* ed. Graeme Gibson.
Toronto: Anansi, 1973.]
THOMAS, AUDREY (b. 1935). *Mrs. Blood.* Indianapolis: Bobbs-Merrill,
1970.
————. *Munchmeyer* and *Prospero on the Island.* Indianapolis: Bobbs-
Merrill, 1971.
————. *Ten Green Bottles* (stories). Indianapolis: Bobbs-Merrill, 1967.
THOMPSON, KENT. *The Tenants Were Corrie and Tennie.* Toronto:
Macmillan, 1973.
[Essay by Thompson in *The Narrative Voice,* ed. J. Metcalf (To-
ronto: McGraw-Hill Ryerson, 1972).]
THOMSON, EDWARD WILLIAM (1849-1924). *Old Man Savarin Stories.*
Toronto: University of Toronto Press, 1974 [1895].
TRAILL, CATHERINE PARR (1802-1899). *Afar in the Forest.* London:
Nelson, 1869.
————. *The Canadian Crusoes.* London: Hall, 1852.
VALGARDSON, W. D. *Bloodflowers: Ten Stories.* Ottawa: Oberon, 1973.
————. *God Is Not a Fish Inspector.* Ottawa: Oberon, 1975.
WALKER, DAVID. *The Lord's Pink Ocean.* Don Mills: Collins, 1972.
WARD, FREDERICK. *Riverlisp.* Montreal: Tundra Books, 1974.
WATSON, SHEILA (b. 1909). *The Double Hook.* Toronto: NCL, 1966
[1959].
WEINZWEIG, HELEN (b. 1915). *Passing Ceremony.* Toronto: Anansi, 1973.
WIEBE, RUDY (b. 1934). *The Blue Mountains of China.* Toronto: McClel-
land & Stewart, 1970.
————. *First and Vital Candle.* Toronto: McClelland & Stewart, 1966.
————. *Peace Shall Destroy Many.* Toronto: McClelland & Stewart,
1964.
————. *The Temptations of Big Bear.* Toronto: McClelland & Stewart,
1973.
————. *Where Is the Voice Coming From?* Toronto: McClelland &
Stewart, 1974.
[Essay by Wiebe in *The Narrative Voice,* ed. J. Metcalf (Toronto:
McGraw-Hill Ryerson, 1972); interview in *Conversations with
Canadian Novelists,* ed. Don Cameron. Toronto: Macmillan, 1973;
Patricia Morley, *The Comedians: Hugh Hood and Rudy Wiebe.*
Toronto: Clarke, Irwin, 1977.]

WILSON, ETHEL (b. 1890). *The Equations of Love*. Toronto: Macmillan, 1952.
———. *Hetty Dorval*. Toronto: Macmillan, 1967 [1947].
———. *The Innocent Traveller*. Toronto: Macmillan, 1949.
———. *Love and Salt Water*. Toronto: Macmillan, 1956.
———. *Mrs. Golightly and Other Stories*. Toronto: Macmillan, 1961.
———. *Swamp Angel*. Toronto: NCL, 1962 [1954].
[Desmond Pacey, *Ethel Wilson*. New York: Twayne, 1967.]
WISEMAN, ADELE. *Crackpot*. Toronto: McClelland & Stewart, 1974.
———. *The Sacrifice*. Toronto: Macmillan, 1968 [1956].
WRIGHT, RICHARD B. (b. 1937). *In the Middle of a Life*. Toronto: Macmillan, 1973.
———. *The Weekend Man*. Toronto: Macmillan, 1970.
WYATT, RACHEL. *The String Box*. Toronto: Anansi, 1970.
YATES, J. MICHAEL. *The Man in the Glass House* (stories). Vancouver: Soni Nis Press, 1968.

Index